WORD STUDIES IN
THE GREEK NEW TESTAMENT
For the English Reader

by Kenneth S. Wuest

1. GOLDEN NUGGETS FROM THE GREEK N. T.
2. BYPATHS IN THE GREEK N. T.
3. TREASURES FROM THE GREEK N. T.
4. UNTRANSLATABLE RICHES
5. PHILIPPIANS
6. FIRST PETER
7. GALATIANS
8. STUDIES IN VOCABULARY
9. HEBREWS
10. MARK
11. GREAT TRUTHS TO LIVE BY
12. THE PASTORAL EPISTLES
13. EPHESIANS AND COLOSSIANS
14. IN THESE LAST DAYS
15. PROPHETIC LIGHT IN THE PRESENT DARKNESS
16. ROMANS

THE NEW TESTAMENT
IN EXPANDED TRANSLATION

Untranslatable Riches

From the Greek New Testament

FOR THE ENGLISH READER

by
Kenneth S. Wuest, LL. D.

WM. B. EERDMANS PUBLISHING COMPANY
Grand Rapids   Michigan

UNTRANSLATABLE RICHES FROM THE
GREEK NEW TESTAMENT
by KENNETH S. WUEST

Copyright, 1942, *by*
Wm. B. Eerdmans Publishing Company

Set up and printed, 1942
Twelfth Printing, April 1978

ISBN 0-8028-1241-4

PRINTED IN THE UNITED STATES OF AMERICA

DEDICATED

To John Adams Scott, Ph.D., LL.D., valiant
defender of the Faith once for all delivered to
the saints, my honored and beloved professor,
who during student days at Northwestern University introduced me to the study of this most
wonderful of all languages, and whose life,
scholarship, and encouraging letters have been
a constant source of inspiration all
down the years.

PREFACE

When one has read all the various translations, each of which brings out some different shade of meaning from the inexhaustible richness of the Greek text, there still remains a large untranslatable wealth of truth to which only a Greek student has access. The reason for this is that in a translation which keeps to a minimum of words, that is, where one English word for instance, is the translation of one Greek word, it is impossible for the translator to bring out all the shades of meaning of the Greek word. It sometimes requires ten or a dozen words to give a well-rounded, full-orbed concept of the Greek word.

For instance, the words "thankworthy" and "acceptable" in I Peter 2:19, 20 are the translation of a Greek word which means, "that which is beyond the ordinary course of what might be expected, and is therefore commendable." Here sixteen words are needed to bring out the total meaning of the one Greek word. What we have in our Authorized Version is an excellent "one-word" translation, and correct. But one misses some of the richness that lies hidden beneath the English word. Again, no translation can bring to the English reader the fact that this Greek word is the one translated "grace" when the writer is speaking of God's grace. And no translation can bring out the richness of meaning in the Greek word "grace" as it was used even in pagan Greece.

Or, take the case of the two words translated "love" in I Peter 1:22, the first one meaning "a love that is called out of one's heart by the pleasure one finds in the object loved, and which is nonethical in its nature, an affection, a liking for someone or something," the second, meaning "a love called out of one's heart because of the preciousness of the object loved, and which is sacrificial in its nature, a love conferring blessings upon the object loved." In the first instance, it takes thirty-three words, most of which would appear in a translation that would do justice to the total meaning of the word, to translate the word adequately, and in the second case, thirty words. The single word "love" used to translate these two different Greek words, is a correct rendering and perfectly proper in the ordinary translation. But the English reader would never suspect that there was so much rich material still in the Greek text.

This is the justification for such a book as *Untranslatable Riches from the Greek New Testament for the English Reader* and its three companion volumes, *Golden Nuggets from the Greek New Testament for the English Reader*, *Bypaths in the Greek New Testament for the English Reader*, and *Treasures from the Greek New Testament for the English Reader*. Where a Greek word treated in this book is presented in a fuller or complete way or in its every occurrence in the New Testament in the other volumes, a footnote will direct the Bible student to the page or pages where the material can be found. Thus, the reader can make a further study of the word should he so desire.

The indexes of all four books are presented in one index in *Untranslatable Riches*, thus enabling the student of the English Bible to quickly find the material he wishes. The four volumes can thus be used as a reference work. The English reader with no knowledge of the Greek can obtain help from the Greek text in the case of approximately 1150 places treated in these books.

K. S. W.

CONTENTS

Chapter   Page

I.   Paul's Doctrine of Verbal Inspiration 13

II. Paul's Last Words to Timothy 22

III. An Exposition of the Greek Text of Hebrews VI 44

IV. Light from the Greek on the Ministry of the Holy Spirit.. 74
     1. The Imperative Necessity of His Ministry 74
     2. The Anointing with the Holy Spirit 78
     3. The Baptism by the Holy Spirit 83
     4. The Spirit of Adoption 90
     5. The Sanctification by the Holy Spirit 93
     6. The Fellowship and Communion of the Holy Spirit.... 96
     7. The Fullness of the Holy Spirit 103
     8. Inaccurate Statements 114

Index of Scripture References covering volumes I to IV
     in this series 121

Untranslatable Riches
From the Greek New Testament

Chapter I

PAUL'S DOCTRINE OF VERBAL INSPIRATION

THE classic passage on this subject (I Cor. 2:9-16) was written to a racial group that stands out in history as the most intellectual of all peoples, the Greeks. They were a race of creative thinkers. The sole instrument which they used in their attempt to pierce through the mysteries of existence was human reason. This they sharpened to a keen edge. But it was inadequate to solve the great mysteries of origins, of the wherefore of human existence, of God, and of evil. Plato, one of their great philosophers, said, "We must lay hold of the best human opinion in order that borne by it as on a raft, we may sail over the dangerous sea of life, unless we can find a stronger boat, *or some sure word of God,* which will more surely and safely carry us." This great philosopher acknowledged that mere human reason was not sufficient to answer the riddles with which man is confronted, and that the only sure foundation for a system of religious truth was, not even the best of human opinion, but a revelation from God.

The man who wrote this passage, declaring to these intellectuals that the Bible has come, not from human reason, but by divine revelation, was himself trained in their schools. He was a native of Tarsus, a city where Greek culture predominated. The University of Tarsus was known all over the world. Strabo placed it ahead of the universities of Athens and Alexandria in its zeal for learning. Paul's people were Roman citizens, and also citizens of Tarsus, which latter fact tells us that his family was one of wealth and standing, for during the time of Paul, only people of wealth and standing in the community were allowed to possess Tarsian citizenship. This

13

explains Paul's statement, "I have suffered the loss of all things" (Phil. 3:8). The city was noted for its intense activity, its atmosphere of what we today call "drive." Paul was not reared in the lassitude and ease of an oriental city, but in an atmosphere of physical and mental achievement. That he had a thorough training in the University of Tarsus is evident from his words to the Corinthians: "And I having come to you, brethren, came, not having my message dominated by a transcendent rhetorical display or by philosophical subtlety . . . and my message and my preaching were not couched in specious words of philosophy" (I Cor. 2:1, 4). He could have used these had he wanted to. He was schooled in Greek rhetoric, philosophy, and sophistry, also in Greek literature. Thus in giving the Greeks his teaching of verbal inspiration, Paul was not looking at the subject from only one angle, that of a mystic who knew what fellowship with God was, and who had received communications from God, but he had had the other side of the problem in the Greek university, where he was brought into contact with human reason at its best.

He begins the treatment of his subject by telling the Greeks that neither scientific investigation nor human reason has ever been able to discover a sure foundation upon which a religious system could be built. He says, "Eye hath not seen, nor ear heard, . . . the things which God hath prepared for them that love him." The context makes it clear that these "things" consist of the revelation of truth, the holy Scriptures. But not only has scientific investigation never discovered this truth, but this truth has not been produced by the activity of man's reason, for he said, "neither have entered the heart of man." The Greek word translated "entered," does not refer to something entering the mind from the outside, but was used of things that come up in one's mind. We use the expression today, "It never entered my mind," meaning by that that the thing never occurred to us. Thus we have the statement of Paul that the truth of Scripture never arose in the consciousness of man, never found its source in the reason of man. Observe the bearing this has upon teaching that finds its basis in the theory of evolution, teaching to the effect that all that the human race knows is the result of divinity resident in man, and that therefore, all knowledge has come from within the race, none from without. After asserting the fact of the final inadequacy of reason in solving the riddle of existence, Paul proceeds to describe the three successive steps in the transmission of truth from the heart of God to the heart of man. These are, *revelation*, the act of God the Holy Spirit imparting to the Bible writers, truth incapable of being discovered by man's unaided reason (2:10-12): *inspiration*, the act of God the Holy Spirit enabling the Bible writers to write down in God-chosen words, infallibly, the truth revealed (2:13): and *illumination*, the act of God the Holy Spirit enabling believers to understand the truth given by *revelation* and written down by *inspiration* (2:14-16).

We will deal first with *revelation*. The first word in our English translation in verse nine, Authorized Version, is "but," and is the translation of the strong adversative particle in the Greek. But the first word in verse ten should not be "but," but "for," since the Greek word here is not adversative but explanatory. Paul explains that the Bible did not come by the way of scientific investigation and human reason, but that it came in another way, by revelation. Then he shows that the very fact that God gave this truth by revelation proves that in the nature of things it could not have been given in any other way, and proceeds in verse eleven to show that this is true. The word "revealed" is the translation of a Greek word which means "to uncover, to lay open what has been veiled or covered up." The word "us" refers to the Bible writers, for Paul is explaining to the Greeks his knowledge of the truth. The Holy Spirit who searches the deep things of God, uncovered this truth to the vision of these men.

Then Paul by the use of pure logic proves to these Greeks the impossibility of discovering God's Word through scientific investigation or human reason. The word "man" in the Greek is not the word which refers to an individual male member of the human race, but is the generic term for man, which includes individuals of both sexes. The second use of the word "man" is accompanied by the definite article which in Greek points out individuality. Thus, our translation is, "For who is there of men who knows the things of the (individual) man." That is, no individual knows the inner thoughts and heart-life of another person. Man is inscrutable to his fellowman.

The word "spirit" in the Greek refers here to the rational spirit, the power by which a human being feels, thinks, wills, and decides. Again, the word "man" in the phrase, "save the spirit of man," is preceded by the article. The Greek article originally came from the demonstrative pronoun, and it retains much of the demonstrative's force of pointing out. Therefore, we translate, "For who is there of men who knows the things of the (individual) man except the spirit of (that) man which is in him." Only the individual knows what is in his heart of hearts. To his fellow-man he is inscrutable.

Just so, Paul says, logic will lead us to the conclusion that if a man is inscrutable to his fellow-man, so God must be inscrutable to man. And just as only the individual person knows what is in *his* own heart, so only God knows what is in *His* own heart. Therefore, if man finds it impossible through scientific investigation and human reason to discover the inner secrets of his fellow-man, it is clear that he cannot find out the mind of God by the same methods. The only way in which a person can come to know the inner heart-life of another person is to have that person uncover the secrets of his inner life to him. It likewise follows that the only way in which a person can know the mind of God is to have God uncover His thoughts to man. Thus Paul has demonstrated to these Greeks the absolute need of a revelation from God if we are to know what is in His heart. The first step therefore, in the transmission of truth from the heart of God to the heart of the believer is *revelation*, the act of God the Holy Spirit uncovering the things in the heart of God to the Bible writers, thus imparting the truth of Scripture to them.

This brings us to the doctrine of verbal inspiration which Paul states in verse thirteen. After the Bible writers had been given the truth by means of the act of the Holy Spirit in uncovering it to them, the apostle says that they were not left to themselves to make a record of it. It is one thing to know a certain fact. It is quite another to find the exact words which will give someone else an adequate understanding of that fact. And right here is where the need of verbal inspiration comes in. Paul first makes the negative statement, "Which things we speak, not in words taught by human wisdom." That is, the words which the Bible writers used were not dictated by their human reason or wisdom.

Then the apostle makes the positive statement, "but in words taught by the Spirit." He says that the words which the Bible writers used were taught them by the Holy Spirit. That is, as they wrote the Scriptures, the Holy Spirit who had revealed the truth to them, now chooses the correct word out of the writer's vocabulary, whose content of meaning will give to the believer the exact truth God desires him to have. This however does not imply mechanical dictation nor the effacement of the writer's own personality. The Holy Spirit took the writers as He found them and used them infallibly. Luke's Greek is the purest and most beautiful. He was a native Greek. Paul's Greek is far more involved and difficult than John's, for Paul had a university training, while John's knowledge of Greek was that of the average man of the first century who knew Greek as his second language but never had any formal training in it. Professor John A. Scott in his excellent book, "We Would Know Jesus," speaks of "the superb control of the Greek language" which Luke everywhere showed, and of the "hard and crabbed Greek of Paul as shown in Romans," also of the flowing language of Paul's speeches recorded in the Acts, which quality is not due to Paul's delivery but Luke's literary excellence.

However, whether it is the pure Greek of Luke, the difficult Greek of Paul, or the simple Greek of John, it is all correct as to grammar and syntax. The Holy Spirit observed the rules of Greek grammar as they existed in the Koine Greek of that time. And the wonder of it all is seen in the fact that John brings to his readers just as precious, just as deep truth, in his simple Greek, as Paul does in his intricate constructions and involved sentences. God the Holy Spirit is above language. Thus we have in the original Hebrew and Greek texts of the Bible manuscripts, the very words that God taught the writers to use as they recorded the truth which they had received by revelation. This is what is meant by verbal inspiration.

Then Paul in the words "comparing spiritual things with spiritual," explains this process of choosing the right word in each case. We will look carefully at the Greek word translated "comparing," for it throws a flood of light on Paul's teaching of verbal inspiration. The word is a compound of the verb meaning "to judge," and a preposition meaning "with," thus "to judge with." It speaks of the action of judging something with something else. For instance, a milliner wishes to trim a red hat with ribbon of the same color. She takes the hat over to the spools of ribbon and "judges" the various shades of red ribbon "with" the hat. She compares the hat with ribbon after ribbon in an attempt to find one which will exactly match the color of the hat. She rejects one after another until she finally finds one ribbon that exactly matches the hat. And that is exactly what the word means, "to join fitly together, to combine, to compound." That is just the procedure which the Bible writers went through in writing their books. As led by the Holy Spirit, they searched their vocabularies for the exact word which would adequately express the truth they wished to record. By the process of comparing the word with the truth they wished to write down, they rejected all those words which the Holy Spirit showed them would not correctly express the thought, and finally chose the word to which the Holy Spirit had led them, and upon which the Holy Spirit had put His stamp of approval. Thus the Holy Spirit allowed the writers the free play of their personalities, vocabulary, and training, while at the same time guiding them to make an infallible record of truth infallibly revealed.

The words "spiritual things with spiritual," are from two adjectives in the Greek. The first word translated "spiritual" is in the accusative case, the direct object of the verb "comparing," and in the neuter gender. It refers to the spiritual truths already given the writers by revelation. The second use of the word "spiritual" is in the instrumental case, the instrumental of association. As to gender this word could be either masculine or neuter, for these two genders have the same form in the genitive through the dative cases. The English reader will please excuse these technicalities. We must look at the context to decide which gender is meant. The two things in the context which are compared and then combined, are the truth revealed and the words which would correctly convey this truth. The words "spiritual things" refers to this truth. Therefore the word "spiritual" in its second use in verse thirteen refers to the words. The gender is therefore masculine since the word "words" in this verse is masculine. Vincent translates this phrase. "combining spiritual things with spiritual words." *Expositor's Greek Testament* translates it. "wedding kindred speech to thought." Alford renders it. "putting together spiritual words to spiritual things."

We come now to the doctrine of *illumination*, namely. the act of God the Holy Spirit enabling the believer to understand the truth given by *revelation*, and by *inspiration* written down. Paul says, "the natural man receiveth not the things of the Spirit of God." The word "natural" is the translation of a Greek word which Paul uses to describe to the Corinthian Greeks the unregenerate man at his best, the man whom Greek philosophy commended. the man actuated by the higher thoughts and aims of the natural life. The word used here is not the Greek word which speaks of the sensual man. It is the word coined by Aristotle to distinguish the pleasures of the soul, such as ambition and the desire for knowledge, from those of the body. The natural man here spoken of is the educated man at the height of his intellectual powers, but devoid of the Spirit of God. The word translated "receiveth" does not imply an active appropriation, but a certain attitude of passive acceptance when favorable, and of rejection if unfavorable. This man, whose powers of apprehension are limited to the exercise of his reason, does not admit these spiritual things into his heart. The reason for this rejection is that they are foolishness to him.

Then Paul states the impossibility of his knowing them, and its reason, because they are spiritually discerned. The Greek word translated "discern" means "to investigate, inquire into, scrutinize, sift, question." Thus the investigation of, inquiry into, scrutinizing, and sifting of scripture truth is done in the energy of the Holy Spirit who illuminates the sacred page of Scripture to the believer. It is "he that is spiritual" that judgeth all things. The word "judgeth" is the translation of the same Greek word rendered "discerneth." The Spirit-controlled Christian investigates, inquires into, and scrutinizes the Bible and comes to an appreciation and understanding of its contents.

The fuller translation of this important passage is as follows: "But just as it stands written; The things which eye did not see and ear did not hear, and which did not arise within the heart of man, as many things as God prepared for those that love Him. For, to us God uncovered them through the agency of His Spirit. For the Spirit explores all things, yes, the deep things of God. For who is there of men who knows the things of the (individual) man, unless it be the spirit of (that) man which is in him. Even so also the things of God no one knows, but the Spirit of God (knows the things of God). But as for us, not the spirit which animates the world did we receive, but the Spirit who proceeds from God, in order that we might know the things which by God have been freely given to us; which things we speak, not in words taught by human wisdom, but in words taught by the Spirit, matching spiritual things with Spirit-taught words. But the man whose powers of apprehension are limited to the exercise of his reason, rejects the things of God since they are foolishness to him. And he is powerless to know them, because they are investigated

through the instrumentality of the Spirit. But the man equipped by
the Spirit, comes to an apprehension of all things, yet he himself is
comprehended by no one. For who knows the Lord's mind, that he
should instruct Him? But as for us, we have the mind of Christ."

Chapter II

PAUL'S LAST WORDS TO TIMOTHY

THE last words of great men are always significant. It was so in the case of the great apostle. He was writing from his prison cell in Rome. It was his second imprisonment. His preliminary hearing before Nero was over, and he was expecting the final trial, and death.

His letter was written in Greek to a young preacher whose father was a Greek and his mother a Hebrew. Paul, a son of Hebrew parents had, besides his training under the Jewish scholar Gamaliel, a well-rounded schooling in Hellenistic culture, the Greek language, Greek philosophy, rhetoric, logic, argumentation, and literature. Timothy knew both Hebrew and Greek. Paul chooses to write to him in the Greek language. It was the international language of the day. Greek was far more expressive than Hebrew. It could compress more ideas and their various shades of meaning into one word, than any other language of that day or since. It is because of this that access to the Greek text of Paul's letter is such a great privilege. If the English language had been in use, and Timothy had read a translation of his letter in that language, he would have missed a great deal that lies embedded in the intricate grammatical structure of the Greek, and which could not be brought over into a standard translation such as the Authorized Version. What he would have read, would have been correct. But much would have been left behind in Paul's Greek. This is the author's reason for offering to the English reader who is not equipped to read the Greek, these word studies and a translation using as many additional English words as are necessary to bring out the full meaning of the original.

How wonderful it is that this letter has been preserved for almost 2000 years just as it left the hands of the writer. While it was copied by hand for 1500 years, yet the science of textual criticism assures us of a correct text. And here are a few lines of that part of the letter which we are to study together (II Tim. 4:1-22), in the Greek in which it was written.

Διαμαρτύρομαι ἐνώπιον τοῦ Θεοῦ καὶ Χριστοῦ Ἰησοῦ, τοῦ μέλλοντος κρίνειν ζῶντας καὶ νεκρούς, καὶ τὴν ἐπιφάνειαν αὐτοῦ καὶ τὴν βασιλείαν αὐτοῦ· κήρυξον τὸν λόγον, ἐπίστηθι εὐκαίρως ἀκαίρως, ἔλεγξον, ἐπιτίμησον, παρακάλεσον, ἐν πάσῃ μακροθυμίᾳ καὶ διδαχῇ.

Of course you say, "It is all Greek to me." Everything looks most unintelligible to the English reader, part of a world far beyond and apart from his ordinary sphere of life. He is quite right in his judgment, for to handle the Greek language and produce a translation which is expressive and yet strictly true to the original, is no child's play. Such a thing is not flung off of one's coat sleeve. The subject is so vast that the longer one delves into it, the more he is impressed with the fact that he has but touched its fringes. A translator of the Greek New Testament should have a knowledge of Greek grammar and syntax, the possession of a vocabulary, the ability to break words apart, add together the meanings of the various words which go to make up that word, and then select a word or words in the English language which give an adequate picture of that word with all the lights and shadows it contains. One needs to know the historical background of the usage of the word in classical and Koine Greek. One needs to know the writer, the purpose he had in writing, the particular way in which he habitually used a word. A translator must study closely the context in which the word is found and select that particular meaning from the many shades of meaning which the word has, which best fits that context. All this, and more is involved in the adequate translation of a word. Over and above all this equipment, there must be a definite dependence upon the Holy Spirit, a comprehensive knowledge of the great scope of Scripture, an apprehension of the great dispensations, an understanding of prophecy, and a consuming desire that the Lord Jesus be glorified.

The work itself is of the most taxing kind. It requires patient, slow, careful research, the consultation of a representative number of Greek authorities, the tabulation of each one's material on each word, and a weighing of that material in such a way as to select the best where authorities differ. After one has fully treated each separate word, he is ready for his translation. With your English translation open before you (the writer is using the Authorized Version), let us study the more important Greek words together. When we have finished our word studies, we will offer the fuller translation.

Verse One. Paul says, "I charge thee therefore." Paul's final charge to the young pastor, Timothy, the one upon whose shoulders he is now placing the responsibility for the care of all the churches and the leadership in maintaining the Faith once for all delivered to the saints, is given in view of the spiritual declension and departure from true doctrine which had even then already set in, and which in the last days would come to a head. The Greek word translated "charge" is a very strong word. In pagan Greek it was used to call the gods and men to witness. It was used in such an expression as "I adjure thee." Timothy had splendid moral and spiritual qualities. But he lacked the dogged perseverance and tremendous moral courage of the great apostle. Hence this strong word. The word translated "before," is a compound of a number of Greek words which together mean, "one who is in sight." It was used in such expressions as, "the case will be drawn up against you in the court at Heracleopolis *in the presence of*," "deliver *personally*," "I gave notice in *person*."[1] It is used of one who does or says something in the presence of someone else, and does it with the consciousness that that one has him in sight and mind. Paul delivered this solemn charge to Timothy, conscious of the fact that he was doing so in the sight of God, and he wished Timothy to ever so regard the charge.

---

1. *Moulton & Milligan Greek Vocabulary of the New Testament.*

The expression, "God, and the Lord Jesus Christ" is in a construction in Greek which requires us to understand that the word "God"
and the names "Lord Jesus Christ" refer to the same person.[1] The
translation should read, "our God, even Christ Jesus," the word
"Lord" not appearing in the best Greek texts. This gives us an in-
sight into the Pauline attitude towards the deity of the Lord Jesus.
He emphasizes the fact here, and in a way in which to defend it against
both the heresies of the day and the cult of the Caesar, both of which
were opposed to the doctrine of the deity of our Lord. Thus, the departing apostle leaves with his young understudy an indelible impression of the basic and large place which the deity of our Lord should
occupy in our Christian teaching and preaching.

The Lord Jesus is described as One "who shall judge the quick and
the dead." "Shall" is literally, "to be about" to do something. The
word is used of someone who is on the point of doing something, and
in Scripture, of those things which will come to pass by fixed necessity or divine appointment. Paul was living in the expectation of the
imminent return of the Lord. "Judge" is from a construction which
speaks of action going on. Thus, the various judgments are in the
apostle's mind, the judgment of the Church, of the Nations, and that
of the Great White Throne, a series of judgments, not one judgment.
The word "quick" has changed its meaning in the years since the
Authorized Version was translated. Today it means "fast, swift."
Then it meant "alive."

The words, "appearing" and "kingdom," are in a construction
which shows the thing by which a person adjures another. For instance, Mark 5:7 has "I adjure thee by God." Paul solemnly charged
Timothy by the appearing and the kingdom of the Lord Jesus. The
Greek word translated "appearing" means "to appear or become visible." It was often used by the Greeks of a glorious manifestation of
the gods, and especially of their advent to help. It is used of the first
Advent in II Timothy 1:10, here of the second. Thus the aged apos-

---

1. *Treasures* pp. 31-33.

tle, expecting martyrdom, puts upon the shoulders of Timothy, the great responsibility which he himself has carried these many years, and solemnly charges him in the presence of God, even the Lord Jesus, and by His glorious appearing and kingdom.

Verse two. The charge is to preach the Word. The English word "preach" brings to our mind at once the picture of the ordained clergyman standing in his pulpit on the Lord's Day ministering the Word. But the Greek word here left quite a different impression with Timothy. At once it called to his mind the Imperial Herald, spokesman of the Emperor, proclaiming in a formal, grave, and authoritative manner which must be listened to, the message which the Emperor gave him to announce. It brought before him the picture of the town official who would make a proclamation in a public gathering. The word is in a construction which makes it a summary command to be obeyed at once. It is a sharp command as in military language. This should be the pattern for the preacher today. His preaching should be characterized by that dignity which comes from the consciousness of the fact that he is an official herald of the King of kings. It should be accompanied by that note of authority which will command the respect, careful attention, and proper reaction of the listeners. There is no place for clowning in the pulpit of Jesus Christ.

Timothy is to preach the Word. The word "Word" here refers to the whole body of revealed truth, as will be seen by comparing this passage with I Thessalonians 1:6 and Galatians 6:6. The preacher must present, not book reviews, not politics, not economics, not current topics of the day, not a philosophy of life denying the Bible and based upon unproven theories of science, but the Word. The preacher as a herald cannot choose his message. He is given a message to proclaim by his Sovereign. If he will not proclaim that, let him step down from his exalted position.

He is to be instant in season and out of season in this proclamation. The words, "be instant," are from a word which means "to stand by, be present, to be at hand, to be ready." The exhortation is for the preacher to hold himself in constant readiness to proclaim the Word. The words, "in season," are from a word which means "opportune," "out of season," from a word which means "inopportune." The preacher is to proclaim the Word when the time is auspicious, favorable, opportune, and also when the circumstances seem unfavorable. So few times are still available for preaching that the preacher must take every chance he has to preach the Word. There is no closed season for preaching.

In his preaching he is to include reproof and rebuke. The Greek word translated "reprove,"[1] speaks of a rebuke which results in the person's confession of his guilt, or if not his confession, in his conviction of sin. Thus, the preacher is to deal with sin either in the lives of his unsaved hearers or in those of the saints to whom he ministers, and he is to do it in no uncertain tones. The word "sin" is not enough in the vocabulary of our preaching today. And as he deals with the sin that confronts him as he preaches, he is to expect results, the salvation of the lost and the sanctification of the saints.

The word "rebuke"[2] in the Greek, refers to a rebuke which does not bring the one rebuked to a conviction of any fault on his part. It might be because the one rebuked is innocent of the charge, or that he is guilty but refuses to acknowledge his guilt. This word implies a sharp severe rebuke with possibly a suggestion in some cases of impending penalty. Even where the preacher has experienced failure after failure in bringing sinners or saints to forsake their sin, or where there seems little hope of so doing, yet he is to sharply rebuke sin. He has discharged his duty, and the responsibility is upon his hearers to deal with the sin in their lives.

Not only is he to speak in stern language against sin, but he is to exhort. The word has in it the ideas of "please, I beg of you, I urge you." Thus, there is to be a mingling of severity and gentleness in his preaching. He is to exhort with all longsuffering and doctrine. The word "longsuffering" speaks of that temper which does not easily succumb under suffering, of that self-restraint which does not hastily

---

1, 2. *Treasures* pr. 70-72.

retaliate a wrong. The word "doctrine" is in the Greek, literally, "teaching." It speaks of instruction. Vincent says in this connection: "Longsuffering is to be maintained against the temptations to anger presented by the obstinacy and perverseness of certain hearers; and such is to be met, not merely with rebuke, but also with sound and reasonable instruction in the truth." Calvin says: "Those who are strong only in fervor and sharpness, but are not fortified with solid doctrine, weary themselves in their vigorous efforts, make a great noise, rave, . . . make no headway because they build without a foundation." Or, as Vincent says, "Men will not be won to the truth by scolding," and then quotes another as saying, "They should understand what they hear, and learn to perceive why they are rebuked."

Verses three and four. The exhortation to proclaim the Word is given in view of the coming defection from the Faith once for all delivered to the saints. The word "endure" means literally "to hold one's self upright or firm against a person or thing." It is a perfect description of the Modernist and his following today. The Greek word translated "sound," has the idea of "healthy, wholesome." The word "doctrine" is preceded by the definite article. It is Paul's system of doctrine that is referred to, the Pauline theology. "After" is from a preposition whose root meaning is "down." It speaks of "domination." "Lusts" is in the Greek, "cravings." These who set themselves against Pauline theology are dominated by their own private, personal cravings. Those cravings consist of the desire for personal gratification. They, having itching ears, heap to themselves teachers. The Greek makes it clear that the itching ears belong to the people. The word "heap" means "to accumulate in piles." It speaks of the crowd electing teachers *en masse,* an indiscriminate multitude of teachers. These teachers give the people what they want, not what they need. The word "itch" in its active verb form means "to scratch, to tickle, to make to itch," in the passive, "to itch." It describes that person who desires to hear for mere gratification, like the Greeks at Athens who spent their time in nothing else but either to tell or to hear, not some new thing, but some *newer* thing (Acts 17:21).

The comparative form of the adjective is used here, not the positive. Ernest Gordon, commenting on this verse says: "Hardly has the latest novelty been toyed with, than it is cast aside as stale and frayed, and a newer is sought. One has here the volatile spirit of the Greek city, so in contrast with the gravity and poise of the Christian spirit, engaged with eternal things." Such is the spirit of Modernism with its teachings of the divinity of mankind, and the relativity of truth, its rejection of the doctrine of total depravity, the sacrificial atonement, the resurrection, and the need of the new birth, catering to the desires of a fallen race. It gratifies man's pride. It soothes his troubled conscience. The desire for the gratification of one's cravings is insatiable, and is increased or aggravated by having that desire satisfied. Hence the heaping to themselves of teachers.

The words "turn away," carry the idea of "averting." That is, those who follow these heretics, not only turn away their ears from the truth, but see to it that their ears are always in such a position that they will never come in contact with the truth, like a country windmill whose owner has turned its vanes so that they will not catch the wind. Notice the active voice of the verb "turn away," and the passive voice of the verb "shall be turned." The first named action is performed by the people themselves, while in the case of the second one, they are acted upon by an outside force. The second occurrence of the word "turn" is from a verb which means "to turn or twist out." In a medical sense it means, "to wrench out of its proper place," as of the limbs. It is used of a dislocated arm, for instance. When people avert their ears from the truth, they lay themselves open to every Satanic influence, and are easily turned aside to error. Instead of being in correct adjustment to the truth, namely that of seeking it for the purpose of appropriating it, these people have put themselves out of adjustment and have been consequently wrenched out of place. They have become dislocated, put out of joint. Like a dislocated arm which has no freedom of action, they have given themselves over to a delusion which incapacitates them for any independent thinking along religious lines which they might do for themselves. They are in much the same condition as those under the reign of the Beast who, because they refuse to receive the love of the truth, are the victims of a strong delusion (II Thess. 2:10, 11). The word "fable" is from a Greek word which refers to fiction as opposed to fact. And surely, the teachings of Modernism are fictional as to their nature, for they have a theoretical basis, the unproved hypotheses of science, naturalism and evolution.

Verse five. In view of this sad condition in the visible church, Timothy is exhorted by the great apostle to do four things in connection with his proclamation of the Word. First, he is to watch in all things. "Watch" is from a Greek word which has the following meanings, "to be in a sober mood, to be calm and collected in spirit, to be temperate, dispassionate, circumspect, alert." All these would pass through the mind of Timothy as he meditated upon Paul's Greek. Second, the pastor is to endure afflictions. "Afflictions" in the Greek is "evils, hardships, troubles." The verb "endure" is aorist imperative. It is a sharp command given with military snap and curtness. Timothy needed just that. He was not cast in a heroic mould. How we in the ministry of the Word need that injunction today. What "softies" we sometimes are, afraid to come out clearly in our proclamation of the truth and our stand as to false doctrine, fearing the ostracism of our fellows, the ecclesiastical displeasure of our superiors, or the cutting off of our immediate financial income. I would rather walk a lonely road with Jesus than be without His fellowship in the crowd, wouldn't you? I would rather live in a cottage and eat simple food, and have Him as Head of my home and the Unseen Guest at every meal, than to live in royal style in a mansion without Him.

Third, the pastor is to do the work of an evangelist. The latter word is the transliteration of a Greek word that means, "one who brings good news." Paul does not exhort the local pastor to engage in an itinerant ministry, going from place to place holding evangelistic meetings. That work is for those specially gifted men called evangelists (Eph. 4:11). But the local pastor should be evangelistic in his message and methods. He must ever be reaching out for the lost both in his teaching, preaching, and personal contacts.

Fourth, he must make full proof of his ministry. The words "make full proof," are the translation of a Greek word which means "to cause a thing to be shown to the full, to carry through to the end, to fully perform." "Ministry" is from a Greek word which speaks of Christian work in general, covering every mode of service. One of the chief temptations of the pastorate is laziness and neglect. Paul lived an intense and tremendously active life. The word "drive" characterizes him perfectly. As the saying goes: "It is better to wear out for the Lord than to rust out."

Verse six. In verses one to five, Paul is urging Timothy to take the initiative because he himself is being called from the field of action, and Timothy must carry on. He says, "I am now ready to be offered." The "I" is emphatic in the Greek text. It is, "as for myself," in contradistinction to Timothy and others. To translate literally, "As for myself, I am already being offered." What he is now suffering is the beginning of the end. The process has already begun which shall shed his blood. What was a possibility in Philippians 1:23, written during his first imprisonment, is now a certainty in his second. The word "offered" is from a Greek word used in pagan worship to refer to the libation or drink-offering poured out to a god. Paul uses the same word in Philippians 2:17, where he looks upon himself as the libation poured out upon the sacrifice, namely the Philippian's service to the Lord Jesus, the lesser part of a sacrifice poured out upon the more important part. Only one who considered himself less than the least of all saints could write in such deep humility.

Paul had had his preliminary hearing before Nero, and was expecting the final one, and death. He knew it would not be crucifixion, for a citizen of the Roman Empire was not crucified. If the death penalty was demanded by the State, it would be decapitation, hence the figurative reference to a libation.

He writes, "the time of my departure is at hand." Someone has said, "The servant of the Lord is immortal until his work is done." Paul's work was over, or Nero could not have taken his life. The word translated "departure" is interesting. The simple meaning of the word is "to unloose, undo again, break up." It meant "to depart." It was a common expression for death. It was used in military circles of the taking down of a tent and the departure of an army, and in nautical language, of the hoisting of an anchor and the sailing of a ship. Paul uses the same word in Philippians 1:23. During his first imprisonment, he was kept a prisoner at the Praetorium, the military camp of the Emperor's bodyguard, but now in his second, it is thought that he writes from a cold damp Roman dungeon. In his first use of the word, it would seem that he used the figure of striking one's tent. He was in a military camp, he was a tent-maker by trade, and he spoke of the human body as a tent. If so, it is probable that he had the same figure of speech in mind here.

The words, "is at hand," are from a word which means "to stand by, to be on hand." It was as if death already stood there. Peter also had a premonition of approaching death (II Peter 1:14).

Verse seven. And now he casts a swift glance over his past life, and sums it up in three sentences, using the figures of a Greek wrestler, a Greek runner, and a Roman soldier. He says, using the first figure, "I have fought the good fight." The definite article appears before the word "fight" in the Greek. The use of the indefinite article in the English translation is unwarranted, and makes the expression appear egotistical. The word "fight" is the translation of a word used in Greek athletics of a contest in the Greek stadium where the games were held. The word "good" refers to external goodness as seen by the eye, that which is the expression of internal intrinsic goodness. It is a goodness that is not moral here but aesthetic, a beauty of action that would characterize either the Greek wrestler's efforts or the Christian's warfare against evil. The words "have fought," are in the perfect tense, speaking of an action completed in past time with present results. Paul fought his fight with sin to a finish, and was resting in a complete victory. What a happy ending to a strenuous, active, heroic life. He says in his colorful Greek, "The beautiful contest I, like a wrestler, have fought to the finish, and at present am resting in a complete victory."

"I have finished my course." The Greek word translated "course," refers to a race course, the cinder path of the present day college athletic field. The words "have finished," are also in the perfect tense. Like a Greek runner, he has crossed the finishing line and is now resting at the goal. His life's work is over.

"I have kept the faith." "The faith" here is the deposit of truth with which God had entrusted Paul. The word "kept" means "to keep by guarding." Again, the apostle uses the perfect tense. His work of safe-guarding that truth is now at an end. He has defended it against the attacks of the Gnostics, the Judaizers, and the philosophers of Athens. He has laid it down now at the feet of Timothy. He, like a soldier who has grown old in the service of his country, is awaiting his discharge. And so he writes to Timothy, "The desperate, straining, agonizing contest marked by its beauty of technique, I, like a wrestler, have fought to a finish, and at present am resting in its victory; my race, I, like a runner have finished, and at present am resting at the goal; the Faith committed to my care, I, like a soldier, have kept safely through everlasting vigilance." All this would surge through Timothy's mind as he read Paul's Greek. Much of this is lost to the English reader, this untranslatable richness of the Greek New Testament.

Verse eight. But his use of illustrations from Greek athletics is not finished. He likens himself to the Greek athlete, who, having won his race, is looking up at the judge's stand, and awaiting his laurel wreath of victory. He says, "Henceforth there is laid up for me a crown of righteousness." "Henceforth" is from a word that means literally "what remains." "Crown" is from the Greek word referring to the victor's crown, a garland of oak leaves or ivy, given to the winner in the Greek games.[1] The victor's crown of righteous-

---

1. *Bypaths* pp. 60-70.

ness is the crown which belongs to or is the due reward of righteousness. The righteous Judge is the just Judge, the Umpire who makes no mistakes and who always plays fair. The words "righteousness" and "just" are the two translations of the Greek word used here. The word "love" is perfect in tense, and is the Greek word for a love that is called out of one's heart because of the preciousness of the object loved. The Greek word translated "appearing" means literally "to become visible," and was used of the glorious manifestation of the gods, here of the glorious coming of the Lord Jesus into the air to catch out the Church. To those who have considered precious His appearing and therefore have loved it and as a result at the present time are still holding that attitude in their hearts, to those the Lord Jesus will also give the victor's garland of righteousness. The definite article is used in the Greek text. It is a particular crown reserved for these. The word "give" can be here translated "award." Thus Paul, the spiritual athlete, his victory won, is resting at the goal posts, awaiting the award which the judge's stand will give him.

Verse nine. After his swift glance down the years of his strenuous life, Paul turns to his present circumstances. He is a prisoner in a cold Roman dungeon, awaiting his second trial before Nero, and death. Great soul that he was, he yet needed and craved human fellowship and sympathy in his hour of trial. How this reminds us of the Man of Sorrows who needed the fellowship and sympathy of the inner circle, Peter, James and John, in His hour of trial in Gethsemane. How real a Man He was, yet all the time Very God. Paul writes to Timothy, "Do thy diligence to come shortly unto me." The words "do thy diligence," in the Greek have the idea of "making haste, exerting effort," and can be translated "do your best." Timothy was urged to do his best to come to Paul quickly. Timothy was at Ephesus, bearing a heavy burden of responsibility.

Verses ten to twelve. Paul's associates who were carrying on the work in Rome, had left. He writes, "Demas hath forsaken me, having loved this present world." The Greek word "forsaken" means "to abandon, desert, leave in straits, leave helpless, leave in the lurch, let one down." This tells us that Demas had not only left Paul so far as fellowship was concerned, but he had left him in the lurch also, so far as the work of the Gospel was concerned. He had been one of Paul's dependable and trusted helpers. Paul said that he let him down. This latter expression, so often heard today, was in common use in Paul's day. Our Lord used it while on the Cross (Matt. 27:46), and Paul used it in Hebrews 13:5. The Greek word is however stronger than the English words. It is made up of three words, "to leave," "down," and "in," that is, to forsake one who is in a set of circumstances that are against him. It was a cruel blow to Paul. Right to the last, his intense nature impelled him to do what he could in the service of the Lord. He was awaiting the executioner's axe. Now, one whom he had trusted, had let him down. Paul was in prison, his freedom of action curtailed. Here was one who had his liberty, and who deserted the Christian work for the world, that world which Trench defines as "that floating mass of thoughts, opinions, maxims, speculations, hopes, impulses, aims, aspirations at any time current in the world, which it may be impossible to seize and accurately define, but which constitutes a most real and effective power, being the moral or immoral atmosphere which at every moment of our lives we inhale, again inevitably to exhale, the subtle informing spirit of the world of men who are living alienated and apart from God." Demas loved all this. He prized it highly, and therefore set his affection upon it. The spirit of the age had gotten hold of him. What a warning example to those of us who are teachers and preachers of the Word. How careful we should be to obey the exhortation of Paul, "Set your affection on things above, not on things on the earth" (Col. 3:2).

Crescens and Titus, others of Paul's helpers, had set out on their own initiative as appears from a small particle Paul uses in verse 12 which is translated "and," but is adversative in its nature, and should be translated "but." He writes Timothy, "Only Luke is with me." The "only" refers to Paul's fellow-laborers. He had many friends in Rome. How beautiful it is to see that the "beloved physician" should feel that his place was beside Paul when the end was approaching. How true to his medical instinct this was; not to depreciate the grace of God moving him in his heart to the same action. What a trophy of God's grace Luke is. Here is a Greek doctor of medicine, leaving his medical practice to be the personal physician of an itinerant preacher, to share his hardships and privations, his dangers, and toil. The great success of the apostle whom he attended in a medical way, is due in some measure at least, to the physician's watchful care over his patient who was the recipient of stonings, scourgings, and beatings, a man whose physical strength was always at the ragged edge of exhaustion because of his incessant and intense work and long difficult journeys. Luke knew all the marks (*stigmata*) of the Lord Jesus (Gal. 6:17) on the body of the apostle, the scars left after the assaults upon his person. He had bathed and tended those wounds. Now, his patient, grown old before his time, was suffering the discomforts of a Roman cell. He had to be guarded against disease. "Only Luke is with me." What a comfort he was to Paul. A Gentile and a Jew, one in Christ Jesus.

Paul writes to Timothy, "Take Mark and bring him with thee." "Take" is literally, "pick up." That is, "on your way to Rome, stop by Mark's home and pick him up."

The word "and" in the Greek text is adversative, and has the idea of "but." It distinguishes the going of Demas, Crescens, and Titus from that of Tychicus. The latter had been sent by Paul to Ephesus, possibly to take Timothy's place there while the latter came to Rome. The "but" implies that Paul had not sent the others. Crescens and Titus had gone to some other field of Christian work, leaving Paul alone in Rome, and without helpers.

Verse thirteen. The apostle asks Timothy when he sets out, to bring his cloak along which he left behind at the home of Carpus who lived in Troas. That meant that Timothy would have to take a coast-wise sailing vessel from Ephesus to Troas before setting out westward toward Rome. The Greek word translated "cloak," is the name of a circular cape which fell down to the knees, with an opening for the head in the center. H. V. Morton, a student of Roman times, and a traveller in the regions of the Pauline journeys, speaks of this type of cloak in his excellent book, "In The Steps of St. Paul." He has seen these cloaks on shepherds in what in the Bible was called Cilicia. They are felt cloaks called *kepenikler*, and are impervious to wind and water. They are so stiff, he says, that the wearer can step out of them and leave them in an upright position. They are made of the tough Cilician goat's hair with which Paul was familiar in the making of tents. Such a coat must have been a great comfort to Paul on his long journeys. Now he needed it to keep out the cold and damp of his Roman cell.

Paul asks Timothy to carry along his books and the parchments. The word "books" is the translation of a Greek word meaning a "book," which in turn comes from a Greek word that refers to the pith of the papyrus plant that grew in the Nile River. This pith was cut in strips and laid in rows, over which other rows were laid crosswise, and the whole was pressed into a paper-like material called papyrus. The books Paul asked for were papyrus rolls. The parchment manuscripts were made from the skins of sheep, goats, or antelopes, or of vellum, which latter was made from the skins of young calves. Even at the approach of death, and in the midst of the discomforts of his dungeon, the aged apostle did not allow his normal strenuous life and his habits of study to grow less intense in their nature. What a rebuke this is to those who, charged with the responsibility of expounding the Word of God, are content with a mere surface understanding, not willing to do the exhausting work of research which only will bring out the inexhaustible riches of the Bible. What a reprimand this is to those who have had training in Greek, and who have put aside their Greek New Testament. What an exalted privilege it is to be called of God to minister the Word. As Alexander Whyte says in his book, *The Walk, Conversa-*

tion, and Character of Jesus Christ our Lord, "That elect, and honorable, and enviable class of men that we call students of New Testament exegesis. Surely they are the happiest and the most enviable of all men, who have been set apart to nothing else but to the understanding and the opening up of the hid treasures of God's Word and God's Son."

Verses fourteen and fifteen. Paul warns Timothy against a certain Alexander. The word "coppersmith" in the Greek text refers to any craftsman in metal. He was a metal worker of Ephesus, probably engaged in the manufacture of silver shrines of Diana. Paul's preaching of the Gospel was cutting into his trade in idols, and that touched his pocket book, and he was out to get Paul. The word "did" is literally "showed," with the idea of, not only "evil words," but "evil deeds." One could translate, "showed me much ill-treatment." The word "reward" does not in the Greek text express a wish or desire. It is a simple future, a statement of a future fact. The word is to be taken in the sense of "will requite." The apostle takes satisfaction in the future punishment of Alexander because of his opposition to Christianity. *Expositor's Greek Testament* has the following to say on this attitude of Paul's: "Was the future punishment of Alexander which Paul considered equitable, a matter of more satisfaction than distress to Paul? Yes, and provided that no element of personal spite intrudes, such a feeling cannot be condemned. If God is a moral governor; if sin is a reality; those who know themselves to be on God's side cannot help a feeling of joy in knowing that evil will not always triumph over good."

The word "beware" is from a Greek word meaning "to guard one's self." It often implies assault from without. The word "withstood" in the original has the idea of "to set one's self against." Alexander set himself against Christianity. It interfered with his business. How this reminds us of our Lord's words; "For what is a man profited, if he shall gain the whole world, and lose his own soul? or what shall a man give in exchange for his soul?" (Matt. 16:26).

Verse sixteen. Then Paul speaks of his trial at Nero's tribunal. It is possible that Nero himself was presiding in person. He speaks of his "first answer." The word "answer" is the translation of a Greek word which literally means, "to talk one's self off from." It was a technical word used in the Greek law courts, referring to a verbal defense in a judicial trial,[1] namely, talking one's self off from a charge preferred against one. Paul was offering his defense against the charges of his accusers. But he stood alone, for he says, "No man stood with me." The word "stood" is also a technical word used of one who appeared in a court of justice in behalf of the accused. No one appeared, to act as his advocate, to advise him as to legal forms, to testify to his character. The last persecution had been so severe, that those who lived through it, dared not appear in Paul's defense. Paul says, "All forsook me." He used the same word when he wrote, "Demas hath forsaken me." Those whom he had reason to suppose would come to his aid, left him in the lurch, left him helpless, let him down.

Verse seventeen. But the Lord did not let Paul down. He made good his promise to Paul, "I will never leave thee, nor forsake thee" (Heb. 13:5),[2] this Lord of his who on one awful day was let down by His Father (Matt. 27:46).[3] He says, "The Lord stood with me." "Stood" is from a Greek word used in Romans 16:2, where it is translated "assist." The Roman saints were to stand by Phoebe the deaconess in whatever she needed, that is, they were to make themselves responsible for all her needs. So the Lord Jesus took His stand by the side of His faithful apostle and made Himself responsible for all his needs. He strengthened Paul, that is, poured strength into him, clothed him with strength.

The strengthening of Paul resulted in the preaching being fully known. "Preaching" refers in the Greek to a public proclamation

---

1. *Nuggets* p. 93.
2. *Treasures* p. 25.
3. *Bypaths* pp. 87-91.

given by an official herald. Paul used the same word in verse one. As long as there had been no public proclamation of the Gospel by Paul himself in Rome, the function of a herald had not been completely fulfilled by him. Thus, Paul brought in a full declaration of the Gospel as he gave his teachings to the court. If Nero sat on the judge's bench, he heard the Gospel from the lips of the great apostle himself.

We now consider the significance of Paul's words, "And I was delivered out of the mouth of the lion." Paul did not mean that he was delivered from death, for he had just written, "my life-blood is already being poured out as a libation." He did not mean that he was delivered from Nero's power, for he was aware that a second trial was awaiting him, and that he would be executed. He was not referring to the lions of the arena, for this could not come to a Roman citizen.

The expression, "I was delivered out of the mouth of the lion," is an echo of our Lord's words in Psalm 22:21 where He while hanging on the Cross prays to be delivered from the lion's mouth, namely from death, His humiliation. Hebrews 5:7 (Greek text) makes it clear that our Lord was not praying to be saved from death, that is, saved from dying, but, out of death, that is, saved from the grip of death, namely, to be raised out from among the dead.[1] Paul's humiliation in these circumstances would be his defeat at the hands of Satan when all his friends had let him down, and he would fail to proclaim the Gospel from the pulpit of the universe.

Verse eighteen. The words, "And the Lord shall deliver me from every evil work," are vitally bound up with "I was delivered from the mouth of the lion." The word for "evil" here refers to evil that is in active opposition to the good. The word "work" in the Greek text has a subjective reference and thus speaks of an action that would be committed by Paul. Thus, the expression does not

---

1. *Nuggets* pp. 30, 31.

speak of deliverance from an external evil personality here, but from a possible evil deed of the apostle's own doing. This is in harmony with the context. Failure to proclaim publicly the Gospel on this tremendous occasion, would have been in Paul's opinion "an evil work."

The word "delivered" is from a very tender word in the Greek text. It means "to draw to one's self out of harm's way." Paul was standing alone before the great tribunal, yet not alone, for the unseen Christ, standing at his side, drew Paul to Himself out of harm's way.

This was the climax of Paul's testimony to the Faith once for all delivered to the saints. He had faithfully preached the Glad Tidings through a long life in which hardships, trials, opposition, illness, heartache, and tremendous responsibility had been the rule rather than the exception; and now, at its close, just before his martyrdom, had he failed in maintaining that testimony to his Lord before the Court of the Emperor, what an inglorious ending that would have been to a glorious life. But God's grace Paul found to be sufficient right to the end of his life. He could now go to a martyr's death in triumph. He had remained faithful to his Lord.

Here are his last words to Timothy, as Timothy read them in all the richness of the Greek: (1) *I solemnly charge you as one who is living in the presence of our God, even Christ Jesus, the One who is on the point of judging the living and the dead, I solemnly charge you as not only living in His presence but also by His appearing and His kingdom,* (2) *make a public proclamation of the Word with such formality, gravity, and authority as must be heeded. Hold yourself in readiness for this proclamation when opportunity presents itself and when it does not; reprove so as to bring forth conviction and confession of guilt; rebuke sharply, severely, and with a suggestion of impending penalty. Pleadingly exhort, doing all this with that utmost self-restraint which does not hastily retaliate a wrong, and accompany this exhortation with the most painstaking instruc-*

tion; (3) for the time will come when they will not endure our wholesome doctrine, in that they will hold themselves firm against it, but, dominated by their own personal cravings, they having ears that desire merely to be gratified, gather to themselves an accumulation of teachers. (4) In fact, from the truth they shall avert the ear, and (as a result) they shall receive a moral twist which will cause them to believe that which is fictitious. (5) But as for you, you be constantly in a sober mood, calm, collected, wakeful, alert in all things. Endure hardships. Let your work be evangelistic in character. Your work of ministering fully perform in every detail, (6) for my life's blood is already being poured out as a libation, and the time of my departure is already present. (7) The desperate, straining, agonizing contest marked by its beauty of technique, I, like a wrestler, have fought to a finish, and at present am resting in its victory. My race, I, like a runner, have finished, and at present am resting at the goal. The Faith committed to my care, I, like a soldier, have kept safely through everlasting vigilance. (8) Henceforth, there is reserved for me the victor's laurel wreath of righteousness, which the Lord will award me on that day, the just Umpire, and not only me but also to all those who have loved His appearing.

(9) Do your best to come to me quickly, (10) for Demas let me down, having set a high value upon this present age and thus has come to love it. And he set out for Thessalonica, Crescens, for Galatia, Titus, for Dalmatia. (11) Luke alone is with me. Mark, pick up, and bring with you, for he is profitable for ministering work. (12) But Tychicus I sent off to Ephesus. (13) My cloak which I left behind in Troas at the home of Carpus, when you are coming, carry along, and my papyrus rolls, especially my parchments. (14) Alexander, the metal worker, showed me many instances of ill-treatment. The Lord shall pay him off in accordance with his evil works. (15) And you also, with reference to him, be constantly guarding yourself, for he in an extraordinary manner set himself in opposition to our words.

(16) *During my self defense at the preliminary trial, not even one person appeared in court, taking his stand by my side as a friend of mine, but all let me down. May it not be put to their account.* (17) *But the Lord took His stand at my side to render all the assistance I needed, and clothed me with strength, in order that through me the public proclamation might be heralded abroad in full measure, and that all the Gentiles might hear. And I was drawn to His side out of the lion's mouth.* (18) *And the Lord will draw me to Himself away from every evil work actively opposed to that which is good, and will keep me safe and sound for His kingdom, the heavenly one, to whom be the glory forever and ever. Amen.*

(19) *Greet Prisca and Aquila, and the household of Onesiphorous.* (20) *Erastus was remaining in Corinth, but Trophimus, being ill, I left behind in Miletus.* (21) *Do your best to come before winter. There greet you Eubulus, and Pudens, and Linus, and Claudia, and all the brethren.* (22) *The Lord be with your spirit. Grace be with you.*

Chapter III

AN EXPOSITION OF THE GREEK TEXT OF HEBREWS VI

A NY attempt to deal in an adequate way with this difficult portion of God's word must be based, not only upon a careful exegesis of its text in the Greek, but also upon a study of the historical background and analysis of the book of which it is an integral part. All correct exegesis is based upon and checked up by analysis. Analysis is to the exegete what a compass is to a mariner, or a radio beam to an aviator. The latter two individuals cannot hope to arrive at their destination without the aid of their instruments. Similarly, no expositor of Hebrews VI can hope to arrive at a correct exegesis of that passage without constantly checking his position by the analysis of the book. Therefore, before attempting the interpretation of the section of Hebrews under discussion, we must lay a comprehensive groundwork consisting of the historical background and analysis of the book. The reader can then check the interpretation of any particular detail by consulting this analysis. That interpretation which agrees with the analysis is correct, and that which is not in such agreement is not correct. The matter of correct interpretation therefore is reduced to a science. This eliminates all discussion as to one's theological background or personal views. The working out of the problems of exegesis upon the basis of the laws of analysis and the rules of Greek grammar, becomes almost as sure a scientific procedure as the working out of a problem in mathematics or an experiment in chemistry. The writers of the Bible, led by the Holy Spirit, wrote within the limits imposed by their context. No scripture statement is unrelated to the context in which it is found. We therefore approach the study of this battleground of expositors with the confidence that we are, to change the figure, playing the game according to the rules, not offering the reader an interpretation colored by whatever theological background or personal opinions the writer may have. It is just the scientific way of obeying the laws governing the experiment and tabulating the facts as one finds them.

The book was written before A.D. 70, but after the ascension of our Lord (Heb. 10:11, 12). The temple in Jerusalem was destroyed in A.D. 70, but at the time of the writing of Hebrews, priests were still offering sacrifices, this fact showing that it was still standing. Our Lord is seen, seated in heaven after His ascension. Thus the date was somewhere between A.D. 33 and A.D. 70.

The book was written to prove that a certain proposition was true. The writer states the proposition in the following words: "He (Christ) is the mediator of a better covenant, which was established upon better promises" (8:6); "By so much was Jesus made a surety of a better testament" (7:22); "For if that first covenant had been faultless, then should no place have been sought for the second. For finding fault with them, he saith, Behold, the days come, saith the Lord, when I will make a new covenant with the house of Israel and with the house of Judah" (8:7, 8); "He taketh away the first (covenant), that he may establish the second" (10:9). The proposition is therefore, "The New Testament in Jesus' blood is superior to and supplants the First Testament in animal blood."

We must be careful to note that the book is not an argument to prove that Christianity is superior to and takes the place of Judaism. The New Testament is the reality of which the First Testament was the type. The type consisted of a blood sacrifice which symbolically gave the offerer salvation, while in reality, his salvation came from the New Testament which necessarily is a sacrifice, even the Lord Jesus at Calvary. Christianity is not a sacrifice nor a means of salvation. Christianity is a result of what happened at the Cross, namely, the Christian Church made up of all believers from Pentecost to the Rapture, together with the doctrines and practices of the members of that Church. Furthermore, the New Testament is a covenant made with the Jewish nation. The latter must be distinguished from the Church. It is not a matter of a choice between Judaism and Christianity with which the writer is dealing, but between the type and the reality, between the Levitical sacrifices and the substitutionary atonement of the Lord Jesus.

Since the argument of the book has to do with the abrogation of the Levitical system of sacrifices at the Cross, called in this book the First Testament (9:18), and the supplanting of the same by the sacrifice of our Lord, called in this book the New Testament (9:15), the concern of the writer must therefore be with reference to the *unsaved Jew,* for the proposition which the writer wishes to prove has already been accepted as true by the believing Jew of the first century, for when putting his faith in Christ as High Priest, it became necessary for him to forsake any dependence he may have had upon the typical sacrifices, and recognize in Him their fulfillment.

To prove to him on the basis of his own Old Testament Scriptures that the New Testament has superseded the First, would result in that Jew going on to faith in Christ, if he is really sincere in wanting to be saved. The author proves the proposition he advances twice, and from two different standpoints. First, he compares the relative merits of the founders of the testaments, arguing that a superior workman turns out a superior product. This he does in 1:1-8:6 where he proves that Christ, the Founder of the New Testament is superior to the founders, under God, of the First Testament, who are the prophets (1:1-3), the angels (1:4-2:18), Moses (3:1-6), Joshua (3:7-4:13), and Aaron (4:14-8:6). After stating in 8:6 the proposition he has just shown to be true, he proves it again by comparing the relative merits of the testaments themselves in 8:7-10:39; first, the New Testament was prophesied to be better (8:7-13), second, it is actual, the First Testament typical (9:1-15), third, it is made effective with better blood (9:16-10:39). Then he proves in 11:1-12:2

that faith, not works, is the way of salvation, and closes his letter with admonitions (12:3-13:25).

In addition to proving that the New Testament in Jesus' blood is superior to and takes the place of the First Testament in animal blood, the writer warns those of his unsaved readers who have made a profession of Christ, against the act of renouncing their profession and returning to the temple sacrifices which they had left, and urges them to go on to faith in the New Testament sacrifice, the Messiah.

He warns them against letting the New Testament truth slip away (2:1-4), against hardening the heart against the Holy Spirit (3:7-19), against falling away (5:11-6:12), against committing the wilful sin of treading underfoot the Son of God, counting His blood as common blood, and doing insult to the Holy Spirit (10:26-29), all this being involved in his act of renouncing his professed faith in Christ and returning to the Levitical sacrifices. These are not separate and distinct sins, but one sin described in various ways, the sin of this first century Jew renouncing his professed faith in Messiah as High Priest and of returning to the abrogated sacrifices of the First Testament.

He urges them to put their faith in Messiah as High Priest. He is apprehensive lest there may be among his Jewish readers some who have an unbelieving heart and who are standing aloof (Greek for "departing") from the living God (3:12). He fears lest some should come short of rest in Christ and die in their sins as the generation that came out of Egypt came short of rest in Canaan and died a physical death in the wilderness because they did not appropriate the land by faith (4:1, 2). Therefore he appeals to them to go on to faith in Messiah. He appeals to them to be followers of those who through faith and patience inherit the promises (6:12). When one exhorts someone to do something, it is clear evidence that the latter is not doing that which is exhorted. These Jews, while making a profession, had no faith, and under the pressure of persecution, were in danger of renouncing the intellectual assent which they gave to the New Testament and returning to the First Testament (10:23, 32-34). The writer urges them to place their faith in the New Testament High Priest (10:19, 20), using First Testament typology. Under the First Testament system, the Israelite would enter the Tabernacle in the person of the priest who would procure salvation for him through a blood sacrifice. The writer exhorts the first century Jew to enter, not the Holy of Holies of the temple on earth, but the Holy of Holies of heaven, and in the same way, in the Person of the new High Priest, by a freshly slain (new) and living way, and to do so in the faith which brings full assurance of salvation, a faith they did not have. He warns them against drawing back from their profession of faith in Christ to perdition, and urges them on to faith in this same Christ, with the result that their souls will be saved (10:38, 39). Finally, he devotes chapter eleven to an argument based upon Old Testament scripture, that faith is the way of salvation, urging them to look off and away to Jesus in faith, a thing they were not doing (12:1, 2).

Thus, the purpose of the writer was to reach the professing Jews of that date who outwardly had left the temple sacrifices, and had identified themselves with those groups of people who were gathering around an unseen Messiah, the High Priest of the New Testament system who had at the Cross fulfilled the First Testament system of typical sacrifices. These unsaved Jews were under the stress of persecution, and in danger of renouncing their profession and returning to the abrogated sacrifices of the Levitical system (10:32-34).

We are now ready to present the detailed outline of the book which is based upon the foregoing historical background and analysis.

I. *The New Testament is better than and takes the place of the First Testament because its Founder, the Messiah, is better than* (1:1—8:6).

1. *The prophets* (1:1-3), since Messiah is
   a. God the Son (vv. 1, 2)
   b. Heir of all things (v. 2)

    c. Creator of the universe (v. 2)
    d. Outshining of God's glory (v. 3)
    e. The expression of the nature or essence of Deity (v. 3)
    f. The sustainer of the universe He created (v. 3)
    g. The Sacrifice that paid for sin (v. 3)

2. *The angels* (1:4—2:18), since He
    a. Has a better name, Son (1:4, 5)
    b. Is worshipped by angels (v. 6)
    c. Is Creator and Master of angels (v. 7)
    d. Has an eternal throne (v. 8)
    e. Rules in righteousness (v. 8)
    f. Is anointed with the Holy Spirit (v. 9)
    g. Is unchangeable (vv. 10-12)
    h. Is seated at God's right hand (v. 13)
    i. Has ushered in a Testament which displaces theirs (2:1-4)
       (1) Warning against letting New Testament truth slip away (v. 1)
       (2) If rejection of First Testament truth was punished (v. 2) how much more will rejection of New Testament truth be punished (v. 3), which truth was spoken by the Lord who is superior to angels, and which was attested by miracles (vv. 3, 4).

    j. Is to be Ruler over the Messianic kingdom (vv. 5-9)
       (1) Angels, being servants, cannot rule (v. 5)
       (2) Adam placed over earth, lost his dominion through sin (vv. 6-8)
       (3) Our Lord has regained it for man, who will be associated with Him in His rule (v. 9)

    k. Is the High Priest who has put away sin by the sacrifice of Himself (vv. 10-18)
       (1) He becomes Saviour through His death on the cross (v. 10)
       (2) This death made possible through His incarnation (vv. 11-16)
       (3) As High Priest for human beings, it was necessary that He become incarnate (vv. 17, 18)

3. *Moses* (3:1-6), because
    a. He is Creator of Israel, Moses only a member of that house (v. 3)
    b. He is Son of God over Israel, Moses only a servant (v. 5)
    c. He is the reality, Moses the type (v. 5)

4. *Joshua* (3-7—4:13), because He leads into a spiritual rest which is better than the temporal rest into which Joshua led Israel.
    a. Warning against hardening their hearts toward the Holy Spirit as the wilderness wanderers hardened their hearts against God (3:7-9)
    b. That generation did not enter Canaan rest (vv. 10, 11)

    c. The evidence of the fact that the recipient is saved is that he re-
tains his profession of faith in Christ under the stress of persecution,
not going back to the First Testament sacrifice (vv. 6, 14)

    d. The recipient will die in his sins if he fails to put his faith in Christ
as High Priest, just as the wilderness wanderers died a physical
death because of unbelief (3:15—4:8). The name "Joshua" should
be in text rather than "Jesus" (v. 8)

    e. Exhortation to enter rest in Christ, and warning against continued
unbelief (vv. 10-13)

5. *Aaron* (4:14—8:6), since He

    a. Ascended through the heavens into the actual Holy of Holies
(4:14-16)

    b. Was taken, not from among men, but from the Godhead (5:1)

    c. Is sinless (v. 2)

    d. Is an eternal High Priest (v. 6)

    e. Becomes actual High Priest through His death and resurrection
(vv. 7-10)

    f. Is the reality as High Priest, which does away with the types of the
First Testament (5:11—6:12)

        (1) The recipients hard to teach and dull as to spiritual per-
ception (5:11)

        (2) They had been instructed in New Testament truth (v. 12)

        (3) They were babes, that is, immature in their spiritual thinking
(v. 13)

        (4) They are exhorted to put away "the beginning word of the
Christ," namely, the Levitical ritual, and be borne along to
New Testament truth (6:1)

        (5) They are exhorted not to lay down again a foundation of
First Testament doctrines (vv. 1, 2)

        (6) They had been enlightened by the Holy Spirit as to New Tes-
tament truth (v. 4)

        (7) They had tasted of that which constitutes salvation (v. 4)

        (8) They had been willingly led along by the Holy Spirit in His
pre-salvation work, thus being a "partaker" (same Greek
word translated "partner" in Luke 5:7)

        (9) They had tasted the Word (v. 5)

        (10) They had seen the attesting miracles (v. 5)

        (11) They had been led into repentance (v. 6)

        (12) Now should they fall away from their profession of faith in
Christ and back to the sacrifices, it would be impossible to
renew them to repentance (vv. 6-8)

        (13) The saved among the recipients would not apostasize (vv.
9, 10)

        (14) The unsaved exhorted to follow in the steps of faith of the
saved (vv. 11, 12)

g. Is a High Priest who actually brings the believer into an eternal standing in grace (vv. 13-20)
   (1) Abraham, the man of faith who was rewarded, a precedent (vv. 13-15)
   (2) God's oath and promise guarantee the believer's eternal retention of salvation (vv. 16-18)
   (3) This salvation made possible by the presence of the High Priest in the heavenly Holy of Holies (vv. 19, 20)

h. A High Priest after the order of Melchisedec (7:1-3)
   (1) Melchisedec, a sinner saved by grace, had no recorded parents, no recorded date of birth or death
   (2) A type therefore of Jesus Christ in His eternal priesthood.

i. A High Priest in a superior order of priesthood (7:4-10)
   (1) The Aaronic priests received tithes (vv. 4, 5)
   (2) Melchisedec received tithes from Abraham, therefore was better than he (vv. 6, 7)
   (3) Melchisedec in type still receiving tithes, whereas Aaronic priests die (v. 8)
   (4) Aaron in Abraham paid tithes to Melchisedec, therefore latter is superior; therefore, our Lord is better than Aaron, being a priest in the order of Melchisedec (vv. 9, 10)

j. Is High Priest of a Testament that offered a sacrifice that put away sin (vv. 11-22)
   (1) The First Testament neither offered nor made anything complete (v. 11)
   (2) First Testament priests came from tribe of Levi, New Testament priest from Judah (vv. 12-17)
   (3) First Testament set aside in favor of a better Testament (vv. 18-22)

k. Lives forever: the Aaronic priests died (vv. 23-28)
   (1) Because mortal, there were many Aaronic priests (v. 23)
   (2) Our Lord because eternal, has a non-transferable priesthood (vv. 24, 25)
   (3) Thus able to save the believer forever (v. 25)
   (4) A better High Priest, because sinless (vv. 26-28)

l. Officiates in a better tabernacle (8:1-6)
   (1) His tabernacle the heavenly one, Aaron's merely the type (vv. 1-5)
   (2) His Testament therefore better than the one Aaron served under (v. 6)

II. *The New Testament is better than and takes the place of the First Testament* (8:7—10:39), *because*

1. *It was prophesied to be better* (8:7-13)
  a. The First Testament faulty in that it did not put away sin (v. 7)
  b. New Testament made with Israel and Judah (v. 8)

     c. First Testament dealt with Israel as with a minor (v. 9)
     d. New Testament through indwelling Spirit brings believers to adult sonship (v. 10)
     e. Under New Testament, all Israel in millennium will be saved (v. 11)
     f. Under New Testament, sins put away (v. 12)
     g. New Testament displaces First Testament (v. 13)

2. *It is actual, the First Testament only typical* (9:1-15)
     a. First Testament typical (vv. 1-10)
          (1) Its sanctuary on earth (v. 1)
          (2) Its appointments typical (vv. 2-5)
          (3) Its priesthood temporary (vv. 6-10)
     b. New Testament actual (vv. 11-15)
          (1) The reality better than the type (v. 11)
          (2) The sacrificial blood better (v. 12)
               (a) Animal blood cleanses from ceremonial defilement (v. 13)
               (b) Jesus' blood cleanses from actual sin (v. 14)
               (c) Therefore, He is the Priest of a better Testament (v. 15)

3. *It is made effective with better blood* (9:16—10-39)
     a. The heavenly Testator Himself dies (9:16-22)
          (1) A last will or testament operative only at testator's death (vv. 16-17)
          (2) First Testament made operative by death of animal (vv. 18-22)
          (3) New Testament made operative by death of Christ.
     b. The better tabernacle purified with better blood (vv. 23, 24)
          (1) Earthly tabernacle cleansed with animal blood (v. 23)
          (2) Heavenly tabernacle cleansed with Jesus' blood (v. 24)
     c. The once for all sacrifice of our Lord better than all the sacrifices of the First Testament (9:25—10:39)
          (1) He suffered once on the cross (9:26); He appears in heaven as High Priest now (v. 24); He will come in His second advent to Israel (v. 28)
          (2) Blood of animals cannot take away sin (10:1-4)
          (3) In view of that fact, our Lord volunteers to become the sacrifice (vv. 5-9)
          (4) In so doing He sets aside the First and establishes the Second Testament (vv. 9, 10)
          (5) Notwithstanding this, Aaronic priests still offered animal sacrifices (v. 11)
          (6) The New Testament Priest procured a finished salvation (vv. 12-14)
          (7) The Holy Ghost through Jeremiah bears witness to the New Testament (vv. 15-17)

(8) The Cross does away with the Levitical sacrifices (v. 18)

(9) The unsaved professing Hebrew exhorted to place his faith in the High Priest Himself (vv. 19-22)

(10) Exhorted to hold fast his profession and not waver between the desire to go on to faith in Christ or to go back to the sacrifices (v. 23)

(11) Exhorted to continue attendance upon the New Testament assembly (v. 25)

(12) Warned not to sin wilfully in renouncing his professed faith in Christ and going back to the sacrifices (v. 26)

(13) For the one who would go back, there remains only judgment (v. 27)

(14) The one who rejected the First Testament was punished (v. 28)

(15) The one committing this threefold sin against the three Persons of the Triune God would be punished more severely (vv. 29-31) ; the sin namely, of

(a) Treading under foot the Son of God, a sin against God the Father who sent the Son

(b) Counting Jesus' blood the same as ours, a sin against God the Son who shed His blood

(c) Doing despite to the Holy Spirit in turning away from His further ministrations, a sin against God the Spirit who had led them into repentance

(16) The recipients are urged to remember the persecutions they endured for their testimony to Christ, and not let them go for naught by returning to the sacrifices (vv. 32-37)

(17) They are urged to obtain justification through placing their faith in Messiah and not to draw back to perdition (vv. 38, 39)

III. *Faith, not works, the way of salvation as proved by instances of First Testament saints* (11:1—12:2).

1. Faith defined (11:1-3)
2. Faith illustrated (11:4-40)
3. Faith exhorted (12:1-2)

IV. *Final Warnings and Exhortations* (12:3—13:25).

1. If these Jews remain under the chastening hand of God and do not seek to escape persecution by renouncing their professed faith in Messiah, that is an evidence that they are saved. But if they do the opposite, that shows they have never been saved (12:3-17)

2. When they come to New Testament truth, they come, not to the thunders of Sinai, but to the grace of Calvary (vv. 18-24)

3. They are warned not to refuse the Lord Jesus, for those who refused Moses were punished (vv. 25-29)
4. General Exhortations (13:1-17)
5. Closing words (vv. 18-25)

One thing more is necessary before we look at the exegesis of the Greek text of our passage. We must indicate its analytical structure. The analytical section we are studying starts at 5:11 and goes to 6:12. It consists of a description of the spiritual status of the Jew whom the writer wishes to reach, of a warning not to go back to the abrogated sacrifices of the Levitical system, and of an exhortation to put a heart faith in the New Testament sacrifice, the Messiah. It is one of the passages found throughout the book containing a warning not to go back to the type but to go on to faith in the reality.

This individual is described as hard to teach and dull of hearing (5:11), one who ought to be able to teach but cannot (5:12), one who is a babe (5:13), who was enlightened, who tasted of the heavenly gift and had been made a partaker of the Holy Ghost (6:4), as one who had tasted the word of God and the powers of the age to come (6:5), and who had been brought to repentance (6:6).

He is exhorted to put off once for all any dependence upon the Levitical sacrifices and to go on to faith in the New Testament Sacrifice (6:1). The first part of this exhortation is strengthened by the warning that should he fall away, that is, renounce his professed faith in Messiah as the High Priest of the New Testament and return to the abrogated sacrifices of the First Testament, he would be crucifying the Son of God. This would be an act which would make it impossible to restore him again to that place of repentance to which he had been brought (6:6). The second part of the exhortation is repeated in the words, "that ye be not slothful but followers of them who through faith and patience inherit the promises" (6:12), this second exhortation to faith being strengthened by the example of the saved among these Jews who showed by their lives that they really had exercised saving faith, the "beloved" of 6:9. We must be careful to note that this letter to the Hebrews is written to the professing church made up of saved and unsaved, but the concern of the writer is with reference to the unsaved. We are now ready for an exegetical study of the Greek text of the passage under discussion, based upon the analysis of the entire epistle, the only scientific way of going about our work. We have spent quite a bit of time and space upon our foundation, but as in the case of a building, the larger and deeper the foundation, the more stable and secure is the superstructure.

Verse eleven. The words "of whom" of 5:11 are from a preposition and a relative pronoun, which latter is in a case form that indicates either the masculine or neuter gender. The last named individual to which a masculine pronoun could point, is Melchisedec. But the writer is not concerned with him in what he has to say in 5:11-6:12. Therefore, the pronoun is neuter, referring to the teaching of the Melchisedecan priesthood of Jesus Christ, a thing which these Jewish readers who were still unsaved, needed to be convinced of, if they were to leave the Aaronic priesthood and its system of Levitical sacrifices. The superiority of the New Testament sacrifice over the Levitical offerings is the very thing which the writer is seeking to prove. He shows that Melchisedec is better than Aaron. Therefore, the sacrifice of Christ is better than the Levitical sacrifices. The words "hard to be uttered" are literally "hard of interpretation to be speaking." It is difficult to make this teaching intelligible to these unsaved Hebrews. The difficulty is experienced by the writer. However, it is not found in any lack in the writer, but in the spiritual condition of the subjects of this warning and exhortation. They are dull of hearing.

The word "dull" is from a Greek word meaning "slow, sluggish." It is used of the numbed limbs of a sick lion, and the stupid hopes of the wolf that heard the nurse threaten to throw the child to the wolves. It is a combination of two Greek words, one meaning "no," the other "to push," hence, "no push," thus "slow, sluggish." These Hebrews were slow, sluggish, stupid, numbed, in their apprehension of the teaching of New Testament truth. This made it difficult to teach them. The difficulty lay therefore not in the writer but in them.

But they had not always been in that condition, as is shown by the word translated "are." The word means "to become." It is in the perfect tense which tense speaks of a process completed in past time having present results. These Hebrews had at one time a spiritual apprehension of New Testament truth sufficiently clear that they saw that the New Testament Sacrifice displaced the First Testament offerings. The writer tells us that also in the words, "who were once enlightened" (6:4). The inability to apprehend was not a natural, inherent, and pardonable weakness, but a culpable incapacity which was the result of past neglect of and a gradual working away from New Testament truth (2:1-3). It was the hardening of the heart against the ministrations of the Holy Spirit (3:7, 8). It was a deterioration of spiritual apprehension on the part of these unsaved Hebrews who had been the recipients of the pre-salvation ministry of the Holy Spirit, who had been leading them on step by step toward the act of faith in the New Testament sacrifice, the Messiah. The use of the perfect tense here tells us that the process had gone on to the point of completion, with finished results. Their neglect had done its work, and they as a result were in a settled state of spiritual stupidity so far as their ability to apprehend New Testament truth was concerned. The fuller translation of 5:11 is as follows: "Concerning which (teaching, namely, that the Lord Jesus is a high priest after the order of Melchisedec) there is much that we can say; yet when it comes to the saying of it, one finds it difficult to explain, because you are become those who are in a settled state of sluggishness, yes, of stupidity in your apprehension of the same."

Verse twelve. "Time" is from the Greek word speaking of time contemplated merely as the succession of moments, not from the word referring to a definite portion of time having limits. The word is in a construction which refers to extension. Thus because of the length of time in which these Hebrews had been under the instruction of teachers presenting New Testament truth, they ought to be teaching the same. The "ought" is one of moral obligation. The word is used of a necessity imposed either by law or duty, or by the matter under consideration. "Again" is in an emphatic position in the Greek and is to be construed with "need," not "teach." They again have need that some one be teaching them, the word "teach" showing a continuous process. These Hebrews had grown so sluggish in their apprehension of New Testament truth that it would require many lessons to do anything with them.

"Principles" is from a Greek word which refers to rudimentary ideas. The word "first" in the Greek text refers to the first in a series, the very beginning of things. "Oracles" is from the Greek word used also in Romans 3:2, and Acts 7:38, and refers to divine utterances. Thus, these Hebrews again needed someone to be teaching them, and the start should be made with the very beginnings of the rudiments of the divine utterances in New Testament truth. "Meat" is from the Greek word meaning "food" in general. Today the word "meat" refers to the edible flesh of animals. When the Authorized Version was translated, it meant food in general. Our Lord said, "My food is to do the will of Him that sent Me and to finish His work" (John 4:34). "Are become" is perfect tense, speaking of a process finished in past time with present results. These Hebrews by their neglect of New Testament truth, and their gradual turning away from it because of the pressure of persecution which they were undergoing, had come to the place where they could only assimilate milk. The word "strong" is literally "solid." Thus, only a liquid diet, milk, the very beginning of the rudimentary teachings of the New Testament could be administered, not solid food, the deeper teachings of the Word. The fuller translation follows. "In fact, when at this time you are under moral obligation to be teaching by reason of the extent of time (you have been under instruction), again you are in need of someone to be teaching you the very beginning of the rudimentary things in the oracles of God, and are become such as have need of milk, and not of solid food."

Verse thirteen. The writer continues his explanation in the words, "For everyone that useth milk is unskillful in the word of righteousness; for he is a babe." "Useth" has the idea of "has for his share in ordinary feeding." It refers to an exclusive diet of milk. Adults drink milk, but it is not their exclusive diet. "Unskillful" is from a

Greek word that means "inexperienced." The word "babe" is not the translation of a Greek word meaning an "infant," such as is used in Luke 2:16, nor from a word translated "child" as in Luke 1:7, which latter word is related to the verb which means "to give birth to," and therefore speaks of a child in its birth relationship to its parents; but from a word which means "immature" as contrasted to "mature." Paul uses this word three times in contrast to a word which means "mature."[1] In I Corinthians 2:6 he says that he speaks wisdom among the perfect, that is, the spiritually mature. But the Corinthian saints were babes in Christ, immature Christians. He speaks of those who are perfect, that is, spiritually mature, in contrast to children, namely, immature Christians (Eph. 4:13, 14). Here he contrasts these Hebrews who are immature so far as their spiritual apprehension is concerned, with those of full age, namely spiritually mature.

We must be careful to note that the Greek word "babe" in itself carries with it no implication of salvation. The phrase, "babe in Christ," as used today, refers to a new convert. Paul's use of it in I Corinthians 3:1 is different. There he refers to immature Christians. One can be forty years old in the Faith and still be immature spiritually. Furthermore, the word "babe" needed the qualifying phrase "in Christ" to indicate that these Corinthian "babes" were saved. Therefore, the word "babe" in our Hebrew passage cannot be made to show that the person referred to is a saved individual. It has no birth relationship idea about it. The analysis of the book and the context in which the word is found require that we understand it to refer to these unsaved Hebrews who because of their neglect of New Testament truth and their turning away from it, have again become immature in their spiritual apprehension of the same.

These who are described as perfect or mature and thus able to partake of solid food (strong meat), are said to, "by reason of use, have their senses exercised to discern both good and evil." The word "use" is translated from a Greek word which refers to a habit of the

---

1. *Treasures* pp. 113-121.

body or mind. It speaks here of the habitual use of the perceptive faculties (senses) which are being vigorously exercised. This results in the ability to discriminate between good and evil, and in this context, good and evil teaching. But these Hebrews had abused their perceptive faculties in rejecting the new light given and turning again to the First Testament sacrifices. Light rejected, blinds.

The translation of 5:13, 14 is as follows: (13) "For everyone whose sole diet is milk, is inexperienced in a message which is righteous in quality, for he is a (spiritually) immature person. (14) But solid food belongs to those who are (spiritually) mature, to those who on account of long usage have their powers of perception exercised to the point where they are able to discriminate between both that which is good in character and that which is evil."

Verses one and two. We now come to a careful study of the two Greek words translated "leaving" and "let us go on." A correct understanding of these is absolutely essential to the proper exegesis of the passage we are treating. The word translated "leaving" is a verb meaning "to put or place," with a preposition prefixed which means "off" or "away." The preposition implies separation and is used with a case in Greek which implies separation. The case speaks not only of the literal removal of one object from the vicinity of another, but also of the departure from antecedent relations such as derivation, cause, origin, and the like. It contemplates an alteration in state from the viewpoint of the original situation. It comprehends an original situation from which the idea expressed is in some way removed. Thus, the basic idea in the verb is that of an action which causes a separation. The various meanings of the word are as follows: "to send away, to bid go away or depart, to let go, to send from one's self, to let alone, to let be, to disregard." It is used of teachers, writers, and speakers when presenting a topic, in the sense of "to leave, not to discuss." In manuscripts of the Koine period, we have as reported in Moulton and Milligan's *Vocabulary of the Greek Testament*, the sentence, "Let the pot drop," and the clause, "not to leave me to be neglected in a strange land;" also an appeal from a forsaken girl to her lover, "Oh, lord, do not leave me." In Matthew 13:36 and Mark 4:36 this word is used of the sending away of the multitudes. *Expositor's Greek Testament* translates it here, "Let us abandon." Alford explains it in the words, "Leaving as behind and done with in order to go on to another thing." To use the word "leaving" in the sense that a superstructure of a house leaves the foundation and yet builds on it, as is done by some expositors, is a case of English eisegesis (reading into the text what is not there). But such a usage will not stand the scrutiny of the Greek exegesis of this word (taking out of the text what is there), nor is it in accord with the historical background and the analysis of the book.

The word is an aorist participle. Greek grammar tells us that the action of the aorist participle precedes the action of the leading verb in the sentence, which in this case is "let us go on." The aorist tense speaks of a once for all action. We could translate, "Therefore, having abandoned once for all the principles of the doctrine of Christ, let us go on to perfection." The act of abandoning is the pre-requisite to that of going on. One cannot go on without first separating one's self from that to which one is attached. The word translated "let us go on" is first person plural subjunctive, which is used for hortatory purposes in Greek. That is, we have an exhortation here. Another way of exhorting one in Greek is to use the imperative mode. There is a classification of the participle in Greek which is designated, "the participle used as an imperative." Our word "abandoning" is an imperative participle. It gives a command.

We come now to the word translated "let us go on." The verb means "to carry or bear." *Moulton* and *Milligan* report its use as "bring" and "carry," in such sentences from early Greek manuscripts as: "Her tunic, the white one which you have, bring when you come, but the turquoise one do not bring," and "Return from where you are before someone fetches you," the words "bring" and "fetch" being the translations of this word. The word is in the passive voice, which means that the subject is passive or inactive itself and is being acted upon by some outside agent. Thus we could translate, "abandoning once for all . . . let us be carried along."

Now what does the writer exhort these Hebrews to abandon, and to what does he urge them to allow themselves to be borne along? Well, what does a mariner do when he is at a loss as to exactly where he is? He checks his position by his instruments. The aviator in a similar situation checks his course by the radio beam. An exegete in a similar situation will consult the historical background and analysis of the book. And that is exactly what we will do. We found that the writer proves twice over that the New Testament in Jesus' Blood is superior to and takes the place of the First Testament in animal blood. After proving this, he shows that faith is the only way of appropriating the salvation which the High Priest procured for sinners at the Cross. In the light of this demonstration, he warns them against falling away. He exhorts them to go on to faith in the New Testament Sacrifice. Having left the temple sacrifices, and having identified themselves with the visible Church, from what could they fall away but from their profession of Christ as High Priest, and to what could they fall back to but First Testament sacrifices?

Thus the words, "the principles of the doctrine of Christ," must refer to the First Testament sacrifices, for these Jews are exhorted to abandon them. Likewise, the word "perfection" must speak of the New Testament Sacrifice to which they are exhorted to allow themselves to be borne along. Our analysis has guided us to the correct interpretation.

A study of the Greek text here will substantiate this. The words, "the principles of the doctrine of Christ" are literally, "the word of the beginning of the Christ." The phrase "of the beginning" does not modify "Christ," for He had no beginning. It therefore modifies "word." The phrase, "the beginning word of the Christ" refers to that teaching concerning Him which is first presented in the Bible. And what is that but the truth concerning His Person and work found in the symbolism of the Levitical sacrifices. The tabernacle, priesthood, and offerings all speak of Him in His Person and work. And this interpretation is in exact accord with the argument of the book. All dependence upon the Levitical sacrifices is to be set aside in order that the Hebrews can go on to "perfection," as we have it here. That the word "perfection" speaks of the New Testament Sacrifice, the Lord Jesus, and the Testament He inaugurated by His work on the Cross, is seen from the use of the Greek word here, referring to that which is complete, and in 7:11 where the writer argues that if perfection (same Greek word) were under the Levitical priesthood, then there would be no further need of another priesthood. But since God has brought in a priestly line after the order of Melchisedec, it logically follows that completeness obtains under the New Testament which He brought in. He states in 7:19 that the law of Moses, namely the sacrificial law, made nothing perfect. That is, the Levitical offerings were not complete in that the blood of bulls and goats could not pay for sin. Neither was their completeness in what they could do for the offerer. But "this Man (the Lord Jesus), after He had offered one sacrifice for sins, sat down in perpetuity on the right hand of God" (10:12). His sacrifice was complete. Thus, the writer exhorts these Hebrews to abandon the type for the reality, that which is incomplete for that which is complete. Before leaving this point, the English reader should know that the expressions, "the first principles of the oracles of God" (5:12), and "the principles of the doctrine of Christ" (6:1), are quite different in the Greek. The word "principles" in these verses comes from two different Greek words. The expression in 5:12 refers to the elementary teachings in New Testament truth, and the one in 6:1, to the teaching of the First Testament where Christ was first spoken of.

But the question arises, if these Hebrews had left the First Testament sacrifices and had made a profession of Christ, why does the writer exhort them to abandon these? The answer is that the Holy Spirit had enlightened them (6:4) so that they saw that the sacrifices had been done away with at the Cross, and that the New Testament sacrifice was the only way of salvation. They had acted upon that and had abandoned their dependence upon these, and had made a profession of faith in the New Testament sacrifice. Their former dependence upon the sacrifices had not resulted in their salvation for either one of the following two reasons. In the case of those Hebrews who lived before the Cross, that dependence was a mere intellectual assent such as they were giving now to the New Testament. And in the case of those who were born since the Cross, their dependence upon the sacrifices was of no avail since these had been set aside by God at the Cross. But under stress of persecution (10:32-34) they were absenting themselves from the New Testament assemblies (10:25), and were wavering (10:23), literally "leaning," that is, they were leaning toward the Levitical system again, and letting New Testament truth slip away (2:1). The result was that their spiritual perceptions were dulled, had become sluggish (5:11), and they themselves had become immature in their thinking along spiritual lines. This growing dependence upon First Testament sacrifices, they were exhorted to abandon, and abandoning these, they would be in that place where the Holy Spirit could carry them along in His pre-salvation work to the act of faith. We must be careful to note that these Hebrews had not yet finally and irrevocably discarded New Testament truth. The tendency was that way. The writer was attempting to reach them before it was too late.

If they would go back to the First Testament sacrifices, they would be laying again the foundation of the First Testament, and building upon it again. This foundation is given us in 6:1, 2. "Repentance from dead works" is First Testament teaching, was preached by John the Baptist, and is in contrast to New Testament teaching of repentance toward God (Acts 20:21). "Faith toward God" is First Testament teaching, and is contrasted to the New Testament teaching of faith in our Lord Jesus Christ (Acts 20:21). "The doctrine of baptisms" (same Greek word translated "washings" in 9:10) refers to the ceremonial ablutions or washings of Judaism, and is typical of the New Testament cleansing of the conscience from dead works to serve the living and true God by the washing of regeneration and renewing of the Holy Ghost (Titus 3:5). The "laying on of hands" refers to the imposition of the offerer's hand upon the sacrificial offering of the Levitical system (Levit. 1:4), and is typical of the act of a sinner today laying his hand of faith upon the sacred head of the Lamb of God. "The resurrection of the dead," an Old Testament doctrine, is more fully developed in the doctrine of the out-resurrection from among the dead (Phil. 3:11 Greek) which indicates that there are two resurrections, one of the saints, the other of the lost. "Eternal judgment" of the old dispensation is in contrast to the "no judgment for the believer in Christ" of the new. Thus, these Hebrews are exhorted not to return to First Testament teaching, but to go on to faith in the New Testament Sacrifice.

Verse three. But coupled with this exhortation is an ominous hint, as Vincent calls it. It is in the words, "And this will we do if God permit." Here are his words: "An ominous hint is conveyed that the spiritual dullness of the readers may prevent the writer from developing his theme, and them from receiving his higher instruction. The issue is dependent on the power which God may impart to his teaching, but His efforts may be thwarted by the impossibility of repentance on their part. No such impossibility is imposed by God, but it may reside in a moral condition which precludes the efficient action of the agencies which work for repentance, so that God cannot permit the desired consequence to follow the word of teaching." All of which goes to say that while there is such a thing as the sovereign grace of God, yet there is also such a thing as the free will of man. God never in the case of salvation violates man's free will. The choice must be made by these Hebrews between going back to the sacrifices or on to faith in Christ as High Priest. But their spiritual declension if persisted in, would result in their putting themselves beyond the reach of the Holy Spirit. This is implied in 3:7, 8 where they are warned that if they desire to hear the voice of the Holy Spirit, they should not harden their hearts, the implication being clear that they could harden their hearts to the extent that they would have no more desire to hear the voice of the Holy Spirit. This shows that the "impossibility" of 6:4, 6 resides in the condition of their hearts, not in the grace of God. The translation of 6:1-3 is as follows: "Therefore, having put away once for all the beginning instruction concerning the Messiah, let us be borne along to that which is complete, not laying again a foundation of repentance from dead works, and of faith toward God, of instruction concerning washings, imposition of hands, the resurrection of the dead, and eternal judgment. And this will we do, if only God permits."

Verse four. And now the writer presents a most solemn warning to those among his readers who would persist in their leanings toward the First Testament and their abandonment of the New. It would be impossible to renew them again to repentance. The Greek word translated "impossible" cannot be diluted to mean "difficult." The same word is used in Hebrews 6:18; 10:4, and 11:6, where it can only mean "impossible." Likewise, the word "renew" must be taken in its full force. *Expositor's Greek Testament* says that it means that those who have once experienced a renewal cannot again have a like experience. The person described cannot again be brought to a life-changing repentance. Repentance is a work of the Holy Spirit on the heart of the one who is approaching the act of faith in Christ. It is usually involved in that act, but can also exist separate and apart from it, as is seen in the present instance. These Hebrews had allowed the Holy Spirit to carry them along to the place of repentance. Now should they refuse the proffered faith by which they could lay hold of the High Priest as their Saviour, and return to the abrogated sacrifices of the First Testament, it would be impossible to bring them back to the act of repentance again. And as we have seen, the impossibility would inhere in their own spiritual condition, not in the grace of God.

In connection with this solemn warning, the writer reminds these Hebrews of all that a loving God had done for them. They were once enlightened. The word translated "once" is literally "once for all," and is used of that which is so done as to be of perpetual validity, and never needs repetition. That means that as these Hebrews listened to the message of the New Testament, the Holy Spirit enlightened their minds and hearts to clearly understand it. The work of the Spirit with reference to their understanding of New Testament truth had been so thorough that it needed never to be repeated for the purpose of making the truth clear to them.

These Hebrews had understood these issues perfectly. The type was set aside for the reality, the First Testament for the New. They were enlightened as every sinner is enlightened who comes under the hearing of God's Word. But as the unsaved in an evangelistic meeting today clearly understand the message of salvation but sometimes refuse the light and turn back into the darkness of sin and continued unbelief, so these Hebrews were in danger of doing a like thing.

They had tasted of the heavenly gift, and in such a way as to give them a distinct impression of its character and quality, for the words "once for all" qualify this word also. These Hebrews were like the spies at Kadesh-Barnea who saw the land and had the very fruit in their hands, and yet turned back (4:1-13). One of the pre-salvation ministries of the Spirit is to enable the unsaved who come under the hearing of the gospel, to have a certain appreciation of the blessedness of salvation. He equips them with a spiritual sense of taste with reference to the things of God. Many a sinner has been buoyed up by the message of the evangelist, has had stirrings in his bosom, has had a pleasant reaction towards the truth, and yet when the decision time came has said, "The world is too much with us," and has turned back into sin.

They had been made partakers of the Holy Ghost. We must be careful to note that the Greek word translated "partakers" does not mean "possessors," in the sense that these Hebrews possessed the Holy Spirit as an indwelling Person who had come to take up His permanent abode in their hearts. The word is a compound of the Greek verb "to have or hold" and a preposition meaning "with," thus "to hold with." It is used in Luke 5:7 where it is translated "partners," signifying one who co-operates with another in a common task or undertaking. It is used in Hebrews 1:9 where the angels are "fellows" of our Lord, partners or associates with Him in the work of salvation. It is used in Hebrews 3:1 where the recipients of this letter are called associates of the heavenly calling, Hebrews who had left the earthly calling of the nation Israel and had identified themselves with the Church which has a heavenly calling. It is used in Hebrews 3:14, where it speaks of those who are partners or associates of Christ.

The word was so used in secular Greek. Moulton and Milligan give examples of its usage in the following phrases: "We, Dionysius son of Socrates and the *associate* collectors;" "Pikos son of Pamonthes and his *colleagues,*" "the *joint-owner* of a holding," "I am unable to *take part in* the cultivation," "Some do so because they are *partners* in their misdeeds." Thus the word signifies, not a possessor, but a partner, a colleague, an associate, one who takes part with another in some one activity. It is so used here. These Hebrews became partners or associates of the Holy Spirit in the sense that they willingly co-operated with Him in receiving His pre-salvation ministry, that of leading them on step by step toward the act of faith. He had led them into the act of repentance. The next step would be that of faith. Here they were in danger of turning their backs upon the Spirit and returning to the sacrifices. Peter in his first epistle (1:2), in the words "through sanctification of the Spirit unto obedience," speaks of this work of the Holy Spirit on the unsaved, setting them apart from unbelief to faith.[1] This word does not at all imply that these Hebrews had been born of the Spirit, sealed with the Spirit, indwelt by the Spirit, anointed with the Spirit, baptized by the Spirit into the Body of Christ, or filled with the Spirit. This work of the Holy Spirit in leading them on towards faith was a once for all work, so thoroughly done that it needed never to be repeated. However, there was nothing permanent of itself in this work, for the work was only a means to an end. This is shown by the aorist participle used, referring to the mere fact, not a perfect, speaking of a finished act having present results. The fact that the writer did not use the perfect tense here, which is a specialized tense, but rather the aorist, which is the maid of all work, points to the incompleteness of the work of the Spirit in the

---

1. *Bypaths* pp. 39-43.

case of these Hebrews. So far as the work had been done, it was perfect, thorough. But it would not be complete until the Hebrews accepted the proffered faith from the Spirit. The incompleteness of the work would be due therefore, not to the Spirit, but to their unwillingness to go on as a partner or co-operator with the Spirit.

Verse five. They had tasted "the good word of God," which is equivalent to "tasted of the heavenly gift," and "the powers of the world to come." The word translated "powers" is used in the Gospels repeatedly to refer to miracles, and is translated by the words, "wonderful works, mighty works, miracles, powers." The word "world" is the word which in Romans 12:2; I Corinthians 1:20, 2:6; II Corinthians 4:4 refers to an age, that is, a period of time character-ized by a certain type of life or economy of government or other social regulating agency. In the passages just mentioned it refers to "all that floating mass of thoughts, opinions, maxims, speculations, hopes, impulses, aims, aspirations, at any time current in the world, which it may be impossible to seize and accurately define, but which constitute a most real and effective power, being the moral or im-moral atmosphere which at every moment of our lives we inhale, again inevitably to exhale, the subtle informing spirit of the world of men who are living alienated and apart from God" (Trench, *Synonyms of the New Testament*). It is the "age," the "spirit or genius of the age." This is the present age in which we are living. The age to come is the Millennial Age. What a change there will be when God the Son reigns on earth personally, and His Chosen People are saved. These Hebrews had seen attesting miracles per-formed, the performance of which proved to them that the New Testament was from God. This was another factor which made their guilt so enormous. It is interesting to note in passing that attesting miracles will again be performed in the Millennial Age when the Lord Jesus comes back to earth.

Verse six. We come now to a study of the Greek word translated "fall away." It is used only here in the New Testament. It is found in the Greek translation of the Old Testament in Ezekiel 14:13, 15:8, where Israel is seen falling away from the true worship of Jehovah. The Greek word itself means "to fall beside a person or thing, to slip aside, hence to deviate from the right path, to turn aside, to wander." Moulton and Milligan give two occasions of its use in the Greek papyri which exactly correspond to its usage in Hebrews. The first is; "If the terms of it (the contract) should be broken or it in any other way rendered invalid," which usage is similar to that in the case of these Hebrews should they break their contract which they made with the Holy Spirit when they willingly became His associates in His pre-salvation work, breaking their contract by refusing His further ministrations and going back to the First Testament sacrifices. The other instance of its use is in a document which speaks of a person who falls back on his earlier interpretation of a verb. How like the act of this Hebrew, should he fall back to his earlier position with regard to the sacrifices. The words "fall away" are from a participle in the aorist tense, the time of action being past time, the classification being a conditional participle. The translation reads therefore, "if they fell away." Paul here presents a hypothetical case, warning these unsaved Hebrews from making such a thing a reality.

Now the writer gives the reason why these Hebrews cannot be brought back to the place of repentance, should they return to the First Testament sacrifices. They would crucify to themselves the Son of God and put Him to an open shame. The word "afresh" is not needed nor is it warranted from the Greek. It was included in the translation from a prefixed preposition to the verb meaning "to crucify." But *Expositor's Greek Testament* makes it clear that this preposition here means "up" and refers to the lifting up on the Cross, also that the compound verb was used and understood by the Hellenistic world to mean only "crucify." Besides, any "crucifying to themselves" would be a fresh crucifixion. The words "to themselves" have the idea, "so far as they are concerned." "The apostate crucifies Christ on his own account by virtually confirming the judgment of the actual crucifiers, declaring that he too has made trial of Jesus and found Him no true Messiah but a deceiver and therefore worthy of death" (Ex. Gk. Test.). "The greatness of the guilt is aggravated by the fact that they thus treat the Son of God" (Vincent).

The words "put to an open shame" are from a Greek word used also in Numbers 25:4 (Septuagint translation), where it implies exposing to ignominy or infamy, such as was effected in barbarous times by exposing the quarters of the executed criminal, or leaving him hanging in chains. Archilochus says Plutarch, rendered himself infamous by writing obscene verses. He put himself to open shame.

All this these Hebrews would be doing to the Son of God if they renounced their professed faith in Messiah and went back to the First Testament. Should they do this, they would render their hearts so hard that they would be impervious to the ministry of the Holy Spirit. They would be irrevocably lost. There would be no more hope for them. Of course, it should be plain that this sin cannot be committed today. There is no temple in Jerusalem, no sacrifices to leave and to return to, no attesting miracles being performed, no question as to the closing of the old dispensation and the opening of the new. This sin is not the same as the rejection of Christ by the sinner today. It is not only a rejection of Christ, bad as that is. This sin involves the relative merits of the First and New Testaments, the abandonment of the type for the reality, the sin of the crucifixion of Messiah by His own people.

Verses seven and eight. In these verses the writer presents an analogy in nature. The abundant and frequently renewed rain, represents the free and reiterated bestowal of spiritual enlightenment and impulse to these Hebrews. One piece of ground reacts by producing herbage good for food. This is the Hebrew who accepts the New Testament by faith. On the other hand, the ground that receives the same rain, but produces thorns and briers, is likened to the Hebrew who being the recipient of the pre-salvation work of the Spirit, yet turns his back on Him and goes back to the First Testament sacrifices, the apostate who can look for nothing but certain judgment (10:26-31).

The translation of 6:4-8 is as follows: (4) "For it is impossible in the case of those who were once for all enlightened, and who both tasted once for all the heavenly gift and became associates (fellows, partners) of the Holy Spirit, (5) and who tasted once for all the good word of God and the miracles of the coming age, (6) if they broke their contract (if they reverted to their former position), to renew them to repentance, since they crucify the Son of God on their own account and put Him to an open shame. (7) For land which drank in the rain that comes oft upon it and produces herbage meet for those on whose account it is tilled, partakes of a blessing from God. (8) But if it brings forth thorns and thistles, it is rejected and nigh unto a curse, and its end is burning."

Verses nine to twelve. We come now to the concluding section of this analytical unit. We will need to remind ourselves again of the historical background and analysis of the book, and the purpose of the author in writing it. He was writing to the visible professing Church made up of saved and unsaved. There is no greeting to the saints like we find in most of the epistles. The concern of the writer is with those of his unsaved Jewish readers who under stress of persecution were in danger of renouncing their professed faith in Christ and returning to the abrogated sacrifices of the First Testament. These he repeatedly warns against this act, and repeatedly exhorts to go on to faith in the New Testament sacrifice, Messiah. The fact that he urges them on in faith, shows that they merely made a profession and were not saved. After issuing this solemn warning in 5:11-6:8, he addresses the saved among his readers and uses them as an example to urge the unsaved on to the act of faith.

He addresses them as "beloved." The word occurs only here in this epistle. It is plural in number, and the word used is the one that speaks of God's love. One could translate, "divinely loved ones." It is clear that the writer is differentiating between the saved and unsaved among his readers in this section, because after holding up the "beloved ones" as examples, he says, "We desire that everyone

of you do shew the same diligence to the full assurance of hope unto
the end, that ye be not slothful, but followers of them who through
faith and patience inherit the promises." These words imply that
some of his readers were not of the class called "beloved" whose
lives showed that they were saved. This group whom he exhorts
here is made up of those whom he warns in 5:11-6:9. He urges them
to follow those who have exercised faith, implying that they had
no faith.

He says that he is persuaded better things of these who are saved.
"Persuaded" in the Greek implies that the writer had felt misgivings
but had overcome them. His conviction was the result of proof.
The perfect tense is used, "I have come to a settled conviction." He
assures them that he is persuaded better things of them than those
of falling away and crucifying the Son of God. He also is persuaded
that things that accompany salvation are true to them. One of these
he gives in verse 10. The work of the Holy Spirit spoken of in
verses 4-6 precedes salvation. The constant practice of these called
"beloved," namely, that of ministering to the saints, shows that the
Holy Spirit had produced His fruit in their lives, and that they were
truly born-again ones.

The writer then uses these as an example for his unsaved readers
to follow. Their lives showed evidence of faith, and the mere professing Hebrew should go on to that act. In verses 13-20, the great
example of faith, Abraham, is introduced to strengthen the exhortation.

The translation of 6:9-12 is as follows: (9) "But we have come
to a settled persuasion concerning you, divinely loved ones, the things
which are better and which are attached to a saved condition of life,
even if we thus speak. (10) For God is not unjust to forget your
work and the divine love which you exhibited toward His name in
that you ministered to the saints and are continuing to minister.
(11) But we are strongly desirous that each one of you show the
same diligence which will develop your hope into full assurance
until the end, (12) in order that you may become, not sluggish, but

imitators of those who through faith and patient waiting are now inheriting the promises."

The sluggishness here refererd to is not sluggishness of apprehension as in 5:11, but a certain slowness and hesitancy about going on to faith in the New Testament sacrifice. Thus as *Expositor's Greek Testament* says: "The writer courteously implies that some already showed the zeal demanded, but he desires that each individual, even those whose condition prompted the foregoing warning, should bestir themselves. He desires that they show a corresponding perfectness of hope."

May we suggest in closing, that we have not touched the wonderful beauty of the Book of Hebrews, namely, the Person and work of our Lord Jesus as High Priest seen in the symbolism of the Old Testament priesthood and ritual. The analysis of the book should help to open up these glories to the humble Bible student. In other words, the sixth chapter is not the Book of Hebrews, but just a rather difficult part that needs careful and thorough treatment.

Chapter IV

LIGHT FROM THE GREEK ON THE MINISTRY OF THE HOLY SPIRIT

The Imperative Necessity of His Ministry

THE ministry of the Holy Spirit is an all-important factor in the life of the Christian. It makes all the difference in the world as to whether a Christian has an intelligent understanding of what the Holy Spirit is ready to do for him in his life and in his service, and what his adjustment to the Holy Spirit should be in order that He may fulfill His ministry in and through the saint in the most efficient way. The secret of a successful, God-glorifying, powerful, sweet, courageous, victorious Christian life is in this correct adjustment to the Holy Spirit on the part of the Christian. The imperative necessity of His ministry is seen in Galatians 4:19, which verse we will look at carefully in the Greek text.

The words, "my little children" are more accurately, "my children." The diminutive form of the word "child" is not used here. These to whom Paul was writing, had been won to the Lord Jesus under the ministry of the great apostle. He says that he is travailing in birth for them. That is, he is straining every nerve and exerting all his pent-up love for them in earnestly praying for them. He is praying that Christ be again formed in them.

The word "formed" in the Greek means "to give outward expression of one's inward character." We use the English word "form" in that sense in the sentence, "I went to a tennis match yesterday, and the winning player's form was excellent." We mean by that, that the outward expression which he gave of his inward ability to play tennis, was excellent. Thus we translate, "My children, of whom I travail in birth again until Christ be outwardly expressed in you."

The verb is in the passive voice. That means that the subject of the verb is passive, inactive, does not act himself, but is acted upon by an outside agent. That brings us to the truth that the Lord Jesus, indwelling the believer's heart, does not express Himself, does not manifest Himself, in and through the life of that Christian. He has given that ministry over to the Holy Spirit. He is the agent who takes of the things of Christ and manifests them to us and through us. Our Lord speaks of this same passive state in which He dwells within the Christian's heart, and the fact that the Holy Spirit manifests Him in His beauty through the life of the saint, in John 16:14. His words are, "He shall glorify me: for he shall receive of mine, and shall shew it unto you." There is a demonstrative pronoun in the Greek text which is not brought out in the English translation. "That One shall glorify Me." That is, our Lord says in effect; "I will not glorify Myself. That One (the Holy Spirit), shall glorify Me." The word "receive" refers, not to a passive acceptance, but to an active appropriation. The Holy Spirit's ministry is to take of the things of Christ and show them to the believer. In that way He expresses the Lord Jesus through the Christian. The Christian's life is a prism in which the Holy Spirit breaks up into its component graces, the beauty of our Lord. If the believer does not have an intelligent understanding of and subjection to the ministry of the Holy Spirit, there is little of the Lord Jesus seen in his life. The Holy Spirit does the best He can under the limitations imposed upon Him by the believer, but He cannot do much under the circumstances. The Lord Jesus will not glorify Himself by His own self-expression through the Christian, and if the Holy Spirit cannot, because prevented by the believer, then the life of the Christian has little in it of the sweet graces of the Son of God. Herein lies the imperative necessity of the ministry of the Holy Spirit to the believer. Dr. Max I. Reich put this beautifully when he said: "If we make room for the Holy Spirit, He will make room for the Lord Jesus." The converse is also true, that if we do not make room for the Holy Spirit, He cannot make room for the Lord Jesus.

Before going on in our exposition of this wonderful verse, may we pick up a golden nugget along our path. The passive voice of the verb "be formed," brings us to this tremendous truth. God the Father keeps Himself in the background and puts forth His adorable Son. God the Son keeps Himself in the background and gives the ministry of glorifying Him to the Holy Spirit. God the Holy Spirit keeps Himself in the background and manifests forth the Son. Observe the infinite humility of the three Persons of the Godhead. The only three Persons in the universe who have the prerogative of putting themselves forward and of glorifying themselves, do not do so. What contempt this pours upon our petty pride, our desire for pre-eminence, our pouting when we are not put forward as we think we ought to be or appreciated as we think we deserve to be.

But to get back to our main line of thought. Paul prays that Christ might *again* be outwardly expressed in these Christians. That means that at one time in their lives He was being outwardly expressed. At that time these believers were in correct adjustment to the Holy Spirit and were the subjects of His ministry. The fact that the Lord Jesus was not then being expressed in their lives, shows that they were not at that time the recipients of that ministry. What had happened to deprive them of the working of the Holy Spirit in their lives? The answer is found in Paul's words to them (Gal. 1:6, 7), "I marvel that you are so soon removed from him that called you into the grace of Christ, to another message of good news which is not only good news of a different kind, but good news that is diametrically opposed to the good news I preached to you, which good news is not a substitute message for the one I gave you." These Galatian Christians had turned from Paul's message of grace to the message of the Judaizers. These latter were nominal Christians who accepted Jesus as Messiah, and as the Saviour of Israel only. They taught that a Gentile could be saved only by entering Christianity through the gate of Judaism. One of the tendencies of the first century was that of religious syncretism, namely, the blending together of several religions. When a Greek accepted Christianity, the tendency was to interpret his new found faith in terms of Greek philosophy. When a Jew came over to Christianity, the tendency was to interpret it in terms of Judaism, his old system of religion. This is what the Judaizers were doing. This is what Paul fought against.

These Judaizers came to the Galatian Christians who were truly regenerated, Spirit-indwelt children of God, and taught that they were justified by the Mosaic law (5:4). Because there was no such thing under the law as an indwelling Holy Spirit who had come to take up His permanent residence in the believer's heart for His ministry of sanctification, this teaching deprived these Galatian Christians of their dependence upon the Spirit, and thus also of the Spirit's work of manifesting Christ in outward expression in their lives (Acts 19:2). This is what Paul means when he says, "ye are fallen from grace" (5:4). The apostle is not talking about their justification. The Holy Spirit had nothing to do with that. Justification is a purely legal matter. The entire context is that of sanctification and the work of the Spirit. He says, "We through the Spirit wait for the hope of righteousness by faith" (5:5). He offers the cure for the condition in which they found themselves, in the words, "Walk in the Spirit, and ye shall not fulfill the lusts of the flesh" (5:16), and then speaks of the result of walking in the Spirit in verses 22 and 23. These Galatian Christians had fallen from grace in the sense that they had deprived themselves of the ministry of the Holy Spirit in which He ministered grace to them, daily grace for daily living (II Cor. 12:9; Gal. 5:4).

The position of these Galatian Christians is the position of those children of God who are not conversant with the teaching regarding the Person and work of the Holy Spirit. They are like those converts of John the Baptist who when confronted with Paul's question, "Did ye receive the Spirit when ye believed?" (Acts 19:2), answered, "We have not so much as heard whether there be any Holy Ghost."[1] This is the explanation for the fact that there is so little of the beauty of the Lord Jesus in the lives of so many earnest Christians.

---

1. *Nuggets* pp. 96, 97.

These are doing their best to live a good Christian life, but their own strength is not equal to the task. The Holy Spirit does all He can for them under the circumstances. Their lives are certainly different from what they were before they were saved. There has been a right-about-face. There is a certain amount of victory over sin. They enjoy the things of God. But as for their lives radiating the Lord Jesus, there is very little of that. The Lord Jesus dwelling in their hearts, will not give outward expression of Himself in their lives. He has given that ministry over to the Holy Spirit. And if the Holy Spirit is not recognized and depended upon for this work, He simply cannot perform it, for, just as Jesus never saves a person until that person recognizes Him as Saviour and by an act of his own free will puts his trust in Him, so the Holy Spirit is waiting for the Christian to recognize His ministry, and by an act of his free will, trust Him to perform it. The Galatian Christians fell from that state of dependence upon the Holy Spirit. Most Christians have never been in that state, and therefore have not fallen from it, but because of their ignorance of this teaching, are not the recipients of His work. It would have been well if the one who introduced them to the Saviour had then introduced them as well to the Holy Spirit. But alas, too often the soul winner himself is not in possession of the teaching of and experience in the ministry of the Spirit to the saint.

The Anointing With the Holy Spirit

There are two Greek words, *aleipho* and *chrio*, used in the New Testament, translated by the one English word "anoint." The former is used exclusively in the New Testament of the anointing with oil for medicinal purposes or for the well-being and comfort of the body in the dry hot climate of the East, or in the case of the application of ointment, for the latter purpose, but with the addition of an element of luxury, as in the case of the woman who anointed the feet of Jesus.[1] The latter is used only of the anointing with the Holy Spirit in the New Testament. It is used in secular

---

1. *Treasures* pp. 122-125.

manuscripts, of the application of a lotion to a sick horse, and of the anointing of camels.[1] The two words for "anoint" therefore refer to the act of applying something to either man or beast, this application being for a certain purpose, and to meet a certain condition.

We will look at Peter's words, "God anointed Jesus of Nazareth with the Holy Ghost and with power" (Acts 10:38). The words "Holy Ghost" and "power" are in the instrumental case in Greek, and are in the classification of "the instrumental of means." This expresses impersonal means, and indicates the means whereby the action in the verb is performed. When the means is a person, another case is used in connection with a preposition. The only deviation from this latter rule is where the verb is in the passive voice, in which case the instrumental of means is used. An illustration of this is in Romans 8:14, "For as many as are led by the Spirit of God." Here the subject of the verb is passive, inactive, and is being acted upon. These are being led by means of the activity of the Holy Spirit. But in Acts 10:38, the verb is in the active voice. The subject, "God," does the acting, and the Holy Spirit, designated by the instrumental case, even though Himself a Person, is here looked upon as a means that is impersonal so far as any activity in the premises is concerned. That means that the element which God used in anointing the Man Christ Jesus was the Holy Spirit. The Holy Spirit did not do the anointing. He is that with which Jesus was anointed. We saw that both Greek words meaning "to anoint," referred to the application of something to a person. Thus the act of God in anointing Jesus with the Holy Spirit, referred to His act of sending the Holy Spirit to rest upon Him for the ministry which He as the Man Christ Jesus was to accomplish on earth. It is a case of "position upon." This is made clearer by our Lord's words from Isaiah 61:1, "The Spirit of the Lord is upon me, because he hath anointed me to preach the gospel to the poor;" (Luke 4:18). Luke quotes from the Septuagint, the Greek

---

1. *Treasures* pp. 122-125.

translation of the Old Testament. However, the same passage in the
Authorized Version of the Old Testament reads, "The Spirit of the
Lord is upon me; because the Lord hath anointed me to preach
good tidings to the poor."[1] The repetition of the word "Lord" in
Isaiah 61:1 makes it clear that the pronoun "he" in Luke's quotation
refers to the Lord God and not to the Holy Spirit. The Holy Spirit
does not anoint. He is the anointing Himself. Our Lord explains the
position of the Holy Spirit upon Him by saying that God placed
the Holy Spirit upon Him to equip Him for His ministry in preaching the gospel. Thus, in the case of our Lord, the anointing with the
Spirit refers to the Person of the Holy Spirit coming upon Him, this
position of the Holy Spirit providing the potential equipment for
ministry of which our Lord was to avail Himself. The anointing
with the Holy Spirit would only become a factor in our Lord's life
resulting in the impartation of power for service as He depended
upon the Spirit for His ministry to and through Him.

We come now to the anointing of the believer with the Holy
Spirit in this Age of Grace. Paul says in II Corinthians 1:21, 22,
"Now he which stablisheth us with you in Christ, and hath anointed
us, is God, who hath also sealed us, and given the earnest of the
Spirit in our hearts." In I John 2:27 we have the words, "But the
anointing which ye have received of him abideth in you, and ye
need not that any man teach you: but as his anointing teacheth you
of all things, and is truth, and is no lie, and even as it hath taught
you, ye shall abide in him," and in verse 20, "But ye have an unction
from the Holy One, and ye all know." We have here the noun form
of *chrio*, which is *chrisma*, and is translated "anointing." In the case
of our Lord, the Holy Spirit rested *upon* Him, for that was the order
in the dispensation of law (Num. 11:29). In the case of the believer
during this Age of Grace, the Holy Spirit is placed *within* him

---

1. The difference is found in the fact that the Authorized Version was
translated from the Massoretic text of the Hebrew Bible, which was the result-
ant text of the critical work of Hebrew scholars from the years A.D. 500-900,
while the Septuagint is a translation made between 285—150 B.C. from other
Hebrew manuscripts.

(John 14:17). His ministry in the believer today is not only for service as was the case in Old Testament times, but also for sanctification. But His indwelling is only potential so far as His ministry is concerned. His indwelling does not at all mean that His ministry is performed in its fullest manifestation and in an automatic way. The believer must avail himself of that ministry through the avenue of trust, just as he availed himself of the ministry of the Saviour through trusting Him. Two of the Spirit's ministries are given here, His work of teaching the believer the Word, and His work of giving the believer an innate ability to know in an intuitive way, things spiritual. The Greek word for "know" in this passage gives us this latter truth. A slight correction is offered in the words "ye all know," not "ye know all things." Thus the anointing with the Spirit in the case of the believer refers to the act of God the Father sending the Spirit to take up His abode in his heart, and this in answer to the prayer of God the Son (John 14:16).

We look now at James 4:5, which reads, "Do you think that the scripture saith in vain, The spirit that dwelleth in us lusteth to envy?" The verb "dwell" is not from the Greek word which means "to take up one's residence," but from a closely allied verb meaning "to cause to take up residence, to send or bring to an abode." How true to other scripture is the usage of this word. The Holy Spirit does not of Himself take up His residence in the heart of the believer. He is caused to do so. In the outworking of the plan of salvation, there is subordination among the members of the Godhead. Here the Holy Spirit, Very God Himself, the third Person of the Triune God, is sent by God the Father, caused to take up His residence in our hearts.

But that is not all. The simple verb means, "to cause to take up residence." A preposition is prefixed to this verb which means literally "down," and gives the idea of permanency. Thus the Holy Spirit has been caused to take up His permanent residence in our hearts. This agrees with I John 2:27 where the word translated "abide" means "to abide" in the sense of "to remain." Thus, the

Holy Spirit never leaves the believer. This means that he is saved forever. To pray such a prayer in this Age of Grace as David prayed (Psalm 51:11) is not in order. Inasmuch as in Old Testament times, the Holy Spirit only came upon believers for the time of a specific service, their salvation was not affected.

But what do the words, "lusteth to envy" mean. The word "lusteth" is the translation of a Greek word that means "to earnestly or passionately desire." The indwelling Holy Spirit possessing all the potential power and help a saint needs, has a passionate desire to the point of envy. Of what is He envious, and what does He passionately desire? The context makes this clear. James is speaking here of adulterers and adulteresses in a spiritual sense, Christians who were not living in separation from the world and unto God. They had committed spiritual adultery in playing false to their Lord and in fellowshipping with the world. They were allowing their evil natures to control them, those evil natures from which they had been delivered when God saved them. The Holy Spirit is envious of any control which that fallen nature might have over the believer, and passionately desirous of Himself controlling his thoughts, words, and deeds. He is desirous of having the believer depend upon Him for His ministry to him, in order that He might discharge His responsibility to the One who sent Him, namely, that of causing the believer to grow in his Christian life.

The anointing with the Spirit refers therefore, to the act of God the Father causing the Spirit to take up His permanent residence in the believer. It takes place just once, at the time the sinner puts his faith in the Saviour, and is never repeated. Paul said to the disciples of John the Baptist, "Did ye receive the Spirit when ye believed?" The Levitical priests were anointed once with oil, at their induction into the priesthood (Ex. 29:7). The same applies to the New Testament priests. It is therefore not scriptural to pray for a fresh anointing of the Spirit for a brother who is about to minister in the Word. Let us pray that he might be filled with the Spirit as he ministers. That is scriptural and proper. God expects us to pray in accordance with what is revealed.

The anointing with the Spirit forms the basis of all His ministry to and in behalf of the believer. Let us remember that it is potential in its nature. The mere indwelling of the Spirit does not guarantee the full efficacy of His work in us, since that indwelling is not automatic in its nature. God's ideal for the indwelling of the Spirit is found in the word translated "caused to take up His residence." Its root is in the word "home." The Spirit was sent to the believer's heart to make His home there. That means that the Christian must make Him feel at home. He can do that by giving the Holy Spirit absolute liberty of action in his heart, the home in which He lives. This means that the believer is to yield himself, all of himself, to the Spirit's control, depend upon the Spirit for guidance, teaching, strength. Then will the potential power resident in the presence of the Spirit in the heart of the believer be operative in his life.

The Baptism by the Spirit

The purpose of this study is to examine the Greek text in order that we may come to some clear-cut, definite conclusion as to the meaning and purpose of the baptism that is related to the Holy Spirit. We go at once to the Greek word translated "baptize," setting aside the English word, and for the reason that the word "baptize" is not a word native to the English language, and therefore has no meaning of its own. The English word "baptize" is not the translation of the Greek word, but only its transliteration. In translation we bring the meaning of a word over into the second language, in transliteration, the spelling. Whatever meaning it may rightfully have in the Bible, must come from the Greek word of which it is the spelling in English letter equivalents. This procedure will do away with any misapprehensions that exist as to the meaning of the English word "baptize." Thus we are on solid ground, and are transported, so to speak, to the ancient past, to the time during which the Greek word was used in the writing of the New Testament manuscripts.

The Greek word is used in the New Testament in two ways. When man does the baptizing, a ceremony is in view. This is the ceremonial usage. When God does the baptizing, that which is in view is the exertion of God's power. This latter usage we call for want of a better name, the mechanical usage, namely, that usage in which a person is said to do something to something else through the exercise of his own strength by means of instruments, whether by means of his own members or with the assistance of some other thing. Since we are not considering here the ceremonial usage, and for the reason that we are dealing with the act of God the Holy Spirit, we will look at the mechanical usage of the word.

In classical Greek, the word "baptize" is used first in the ninth book of the Odyssey, where the hissing of the burning eye of the Cyclops is compared to the sound of water where a smith dips, "baptizes" a piece of iron, tempering it. Euripedes uses the word of a ship which goes down in the water and does not come back to the surface. In Xenophon's *Anabasis* we have an instance where the word "baptize" is used of the practice of Greek soldiers in placing the points of their spears in a bowl of blood before going to war. We see in this last instance a ceremonial usage also. This was a ceremony they observed, its observance involving the mechanical meaning of the word 'baptize," that of "placing in."

In secular documents of the Koine period, which documents are written in the same kind of Greek that is used in the New Testament, Moulton and Milligan report the following mechanical usages: a *submerged* boat, a person *overwhelmed* in calamities.

In the Septuagint, the translation of the Old Testament written in Koine Greek, the same type of Greek that is found in the secular documents and in the New Testament, we have in Leviticus 4:6, "And the priest shall dip his finger in the blood, and sprinkle of the blood seven times before the Lord," where "dip" is the translation of the Greek word "baptize," and "sprinkle" is the rendering of another Greek word, the word "dip" referring to the action of placing the finger in the blood, a purely mechanical usage here, and the second word speaking of the ritualism of sprinkling the blood.

In the New Testament, a purely mechanical usage is seen where the rich man asks that Lazarus dip his finger in water and cool his tongue (Luke 16:24), also in the case where our Lord dips the sop (John 13:26), and again, where He wears a vesture dipped in blood (Rev. 19:13), the verb in these three instances being *bapto,* a related word to *baptizo,* the verb usually used in the New Testament and translated "baptize."

The mechanical usage of the word as seen from the above illustrations resolves itself into the following definition of the Greek word "baptize:" "The introduction or placing of a person or thing into a new environment or into union with something else so as to alter its condition or its relationship to its previous environment or condition." The translation is *"to place into,"* or *"to introduce into."* These ideas were in the mind of the Greek as he used the word in its mechanical usage.[1]

We are now ready to consider the meaning and purpose of the baptism by the Spirit. We will look at the Greek text of I Corinthians 12:13, "By one Spirit are we all baptized into one body." The body here is clearly the Mystical Body of Christ of which He is the Head and all believers from Pentecost to the Rapture, namely, from the time the Church was formed until the Church is taken up to Heaven at the descent of the Lord into the air, are members. The word "Spirit" is in the instrumental case in Greek. Personal agency is expressed occasionally by the instrumental case. At such times the verb is always in the passive or middle voice. The Greek construction here follows this rule of Greek grammar. The personal agent in this case who does the baptizing is the Holy Spirit. He places or introduces the believing sinner into the Body of which the Lord Jesus is the living Head. We could translate, "By means of the

---

1. *Treasures* pp. 83-87.

personal agency of one Spirit, we all were placed in one body." The verb is in the past tense, referring to a past action, and is aorist, referring to a once-for-all act. This occurred potentially to all believers of this Age of Grace at Pentecost. It is the fulfillment of our Lord's words, "Ye shall be baptized with the Holy Ghost not many days hence" (Acts 1:5). Thus, the meaning of the Greek word, *"to place"* or *"introduce into,"* gives us the purpose of the baptism by means of the Spirit, namely, the introduction of a believing sinner into the body of Christ. In Romans 6:3[1] and Galatians 3:27, we have this same operation of the Spirit, but instead of speaking of the introduction of the believing sinner into the Body, Paul speaks of the placing of that believer into vital union with the Head of the Body.

This brings us to a careful distinction which we must make. It is not the baptism with the Spirit or of the Spirit, in the sense that the Holy Spirit is the element which is applied to us. It is the baptism by the Spirit. This baptism does not bring the Spirit to us in the sense that God places the Spirit upon or in us. Rather, this baptism brings the believer into vital union with Jesus Christ. This means that the baptism by the Spirit is not for power, for in this baptism there is nothing applied to or given the believer. He, the believer, is placed into the Body of Christ. It is the baptism with the Spirit in the sense that God the Father does the baptizing through His personal agent, the Holy Spirit.

We will study the passages where the expression "baptize with the Holy Spirit" occurs. In Matthew 3:11 we have John the Baptist saying, "I indeed baptize you with water because of repentance[2] . . . He shall baptize you with the Holy Ghost, and with fire." The word "with" is from a preposition which is used with the locative and instrumental cases in Greek. The particular classification of the locative here is "the locative of place." The limits here are spatial.

---

1. *Treasures* pp. 83-87.
2. *Treasures* pp. 76-78.

John said literally, "I place you in water." His introduction of the believer into water is because of his repentance. It is the believer's outward visible testimony of an inward fact, his repentance. Here we have the mechanical usage of the word. But the instrumental can also be seen in this construction, "the instrumental of means," showing the impersonal means whereby the action of the verb is performed. And here we have the ceremonial usage of the word "baptize." Not only did John place them in water, but this placing in water was a ceremony or a rite. He not only baptized them into the water, but he baptized them by means of or with the water. The water was the element with or by which the believer was baptized.

But when we come to the phrase, "baptized with the Spirit," we find that the Greek grammatical construction will not allow us to interpret it as meaning that the Holy Spirit is the element with which we are baptized, as water is the element with which the believer is baptized in the ceremony of water baptism. We have the same case here as in the phrase "baptize with water," the locative. But here the limits indicated by the locative case are not spatial but logical. That is, the locative case, the case which shows the location within the con-fines of which the action in the verb takes place, is not used here with reference to a certain location in space like the Jordan River. It has nothing to do here with any limits in space. The limits indi-cated are not spatial because the Holy Spirit is not a substance occu-pying space. They are logical because the Holy Spirit is a Person. Thus we have "the locative of sphere" which confines one idea within the bounds of another. An action is limited within the confines of an idea rather than within those of a place. Therefore, the classifi-cation, "locative of place" will not apply here, and since it does not apply in this case, the Holy Spirit is not the element into which and with which we are baptized. Therefore the phrase, "baptized with the Spirit" does not mean that in this baptism, the Holy Spirit is applied to the believer as water is applied in the case of water baptism. In other words, there is no application of the Holy Spirit to the believer. He is not given to the believer by virtue of this baptism. We saw that it was the anointing with the Spirit which referred to the act of God the Father causing the Spirit to take up His permanent residence in the believer. Since there is no application of the Spirit in baptism, there is no power imparted in the act of baptizing with the Spirit. This baptism is only for the purpose of uniting the believing sinner with the Head of the Body, Christ Jesus, and thus making him a member of that Body.

The classification of the locative here is "the locative of sphere," since the limits imposed are logical. It is the "confining of one idea within the bounds of another, thus indicating the sphere within which the former idea is to be applied."[1] Examples of this classification in the New Testament are, "Ye have become babes in hearing" (Heb. 5:11), where the word "babes" is limited and thus defined by the qualifying phrase "in hearing." That is, they were not babes in the physical or mental sense. But their hearing of the Word was like that of a child, immature: "He was made strong in faith" (Rom. 4:20), where the meaning is that he was made strong, not here in body or mind, but with reference to his faith. His faith was made strong: "Blessed are the pure in heart," (Matt. 5:8), where our Lord is speaking, not of ceremonial purity such as the religious leaders of Israel were so punctilious about, but of purity of heart, pure in the sphere of the heart. One could render these phrases, "babes in the sphere of hearing," "strong in the sphere of faith," and "pure in the sphere of the heart." Thus we have, "He shall baptize you in the sphere of the Spirit." Here the word "Spirit" sets a limit upon the act of baptism. John is drawing a contrast between his baptism, and our Lord's. John's was into and by means of water, a ceremony. Our Lord's was to be with reference to the Spirit. A baptism with reference to the Spirit is a baptism in which the Holy Spirit is the sole agent. This baptism is limited to His sphere of operations. It is a baptism effected by means of His working. The Spirit baptism to which John referred is the same one

----

1. Dana and Mantey, *Manual Grammar of the Greek New Testament*, pp. 86-88.

which Paul mentions in I Corinthians 12:13. It is a baptism with the Spirit in the sense that it is connected, not with water, but with the Spirit who Himself does the baptizing. The other places where the word "baptize" is used with the phrase "with the Holy Spirit" and where exactly the same Greek construction is found are Luke 3:16; John 1:33; Acts 1:5, 11:16. Mark 1:8 has the same words in the English, and the construction is the locative case in Greek, but the preposition is left out, which latter fact does not affect the classification, "locative of place or sphere," as the case might be. While the preposition in the Greek here is used also with the instrumental case, and the case ending of the noun could also be instrumental, the classification "instrumental of means," could not be used here, since the rules of Greek grammar require a passive or middle voice verb in this construction where a personal agent is involved. This kind of a verb is not found in the passages quoted from Matthew to Acts, but is found in I Corinthians 12:13. Therefore our rendering "baptized by means of the Spirit," is correct for the Corinthians passage but not correct for the others commented upon.

The phrase "with the Spirit" therefore defines what baptism is referred to, and the words, "by means of the Spirit," speak of the fact that the Holy Spirit is the divine Agent who Himself baptizes, the purpose of which baptism is to place the believing sinner into vital union with Jesus Christ and thus make him a member of the Body of which Christ is the living Head.

The reader will observe that our study of the significance of Spirit baptism has been based upon a careful adherence to the rules of Greek grammar. This is a most scientific method of interpretation. It is a most sure method. A. T. Robertson quotes Dr. A. M. Fairbairn as saying, "He is no theologian who is not first a grammarian." All correct theology must pay careful attention to the grammer of the Greek text, for a person is correctly understood only when his hearer or reader applies the rules of grammar which the speaker or writer uses. The Holy Spirit adheres to the grammar rules and idioms of the Koine Greek of the time when the New Testament was written. It is for us to learn those rules and interpret the Greek text accordingly. Then an interpreter of Scripture is on perfectly solid ground. He is far less likely to make a mistake in interpretation when using the Greek than when using a translation.

The Spirit of Adoption

Paul tells us that we have received the Spirit of adoption (Rom. 8:15). It is clear that the Holy Spirit is referred to here. But what does the qualifying phrase, "of adoption" mean? We will look at the Greek text. The word "adoption" is a noun of action. It is in the genitive case. We have here a construction which is called "the subjective genitive," in which the noun of action bears the same relationship to the word defined as the verb of a sentence does to the subject. The word "Spirit" would in this instance be the subject, and the word "adoption," the verb. Thus, it is the Holy Spirit who performs the act of adopting. He is in that sense the Spirit of adoption.

The Greek word translated "adoption" is made of two words, a word meaning "to place," and the word "son," its total meaning being "to place as a son." *Expositor's Greek Testament* has the following to say about this word; "It is a term of *relation*, expressing our sonship in respect of *standing*. It appears to be taken from the Roman custom with which Paul could not fail to be acquainted. Among the Jews there were cases of informal adoption, as in the instance of Mordecai and Esther (Esther 2:7). But adoption in the sense of the legal transference of a child to a family to which it did not belong by birth had no place in the Jewish law. In Roman law, on the other hand, provision was made for the transaction known as *adoptio*, the taking of a child who was not one's child by birth, to be his son, and *arrogatio*, the transference of a son who was independent, as by the death of his proper father, to another father by solemn public act of the people. Thus among the Romans a citizen might receive a child who was not his own by birth into his family and give him his name, but he could do so only by a formal act, attested by witnesses, and the son thus adopted had in all its entirety the position of a child by birth, with all the rights and all the obligations pertaining to that. By 'adoption' therefore, Paul does not mean the bestowal of the full privileges of the family on those who are sons by nature, but the acceptance into the family of those who do not by nature belong to it, and the placing of those who are not sons originally and by right in the relation proper to those who are sons by birth. Hence *huiothesia* (adoption) is never affirmed of Christ; for He alone is Son of God by nature. So Paul regards our sonship, not as lying in the natural relation in which men stand to God as His children, but as implying a new relation of grace, founded on a covenant relation to God and on the work of Christ (Gal. 4:5). The word seems to distinguish those who are made sons by an act of grace from the only-begotten Son of God . . . But the act of grace is not one which makes only an outward difference in our position; it is accomplished in the giving of a spirit (the Holy Spirit) which creates in us a new nature . . . We have not only the status, but the heart of sons."

There are two words used in the Greek New Testament relative to the place of the believer in God's family. One is *teknon*, which comes from *tikto* which means "to bear, to give birth to." Its proper translation is "child" or "born one." It speaks of a child of God in his birth-relationship. The other word is *huios*, the word used in the Greek word "adoption." This word speaks of a child of God in his legal relationship to God in His family. Under Roman law, the only thing that stood in the way of a person adopting a child not his own, was the fact that the child did not come of his own flesh and blood. This obstacle was surmounted by the fact that the law gave him the right to make the child his own if he fulfilled the proper legal requirements. But under the divine government of the universe, there were two things that stood in God's way of making human beings His children, the fact that they were not His children by birth and the fact that they were law-breakers. The first could easily have been remedied by regeneration, but the thing that stood in the way of this act of mercy on God's part was the fact that human beings are sinners, and God's justice demands that sin be paid for before mercy can be righteously bestowed. This is clearly recognized in John 1:12 where the Greek word translated "power" was a technical expression used in the law courts for a legal right to be or do something. The word "sons" is not from our word *huios* here but from *teknon,* and should be translated "children." To those who received the Lord Jesus as their Saviour, as the One who died in their stead on the Cross, thus satisfying the justice of God in view of man's sin, God gave the legal right to become His children. Regeneration is therefore dependent upon justification, since an act of mercy in a law court can only be justly based upon the fact of the law being satisfied in the punishment of the crime committed. In human law courts this is impossible, for the prisoner cannot be punished and be set free at the same time. And the judge certainly will not step down from the bench and take upon himself the penalty which he justly imposed upon the prisoner. But praise be to the Lord, it happened in the law court of the universe. God the Judge stepped down from His judgment bench, and at Calvary paid the sinner's penalty, thus satisfying His justice, and procuring for sinful man a legal right to receive the mercy of God. Thus, nothing stands in the way of a just God regenerating a believing sinner and placing him as His son in His family. The Holy Spirit as the Spirit of adoption regenerates the believing sinner and places him as a child of God in a legal standing in God's family, having all the privileges and rights of God's only-begotten Son. Think of it, to occupy a place in God's family in which He loves us just as much as He loves His only-begotten Son. Think of it, to have a place in God's family just as eternal and secure as His only-begotten Son. Think of it, to have a place in God's family in which all the loveliness of God's Son is ours. The Spirit of adoption is therefore the legal representative of God, so to speak, imparting to us the divine nature and placing us in the family of God, doing all this in accordance with the eternal and unchanging laws of God.

The Sanctification by the Holy Spirit

In the work of sanctification, the Holy Spirit has a two-fold ministry, one to the unsaved, another to the saved. The first is called positional sanctification, and refers to the work of the Spirit in bringing a lost sinner to the act of faith in the Lord Jesus as Saviour. The second is called progressive sanctification, and speaks of the work of the Spirit causing the Christian to grow in the knowledge and likeness of the Lord Jesus.

We will look at positional sanctification first. In I Peter 1:2 we have the words, "Elect according to the foreknowledge of God the Father through sanctification of the Spirit unto obedience and sprinkling of the blood of Jesus Christ." The first step in the salvation of a sinner is his election by God the Father, this election, or selection, as the word can be translated, is dominated by the foreknowledge of God the Father. The word "sanctification" is in a grammatical classification in the Greek called the "locative of sphere." This choice of the sinner was therefore in the sphere of the sanctification of the Spirit. That is, the choice of the sinner was to the end that he might be included in the work of the Spirit in sanctification. The word "sanctify" in the Greek means "to set apart," and the word "sanctification" refers to the setting apart process. The words "sanctification of the Spirit" are in a construction in the Greek called the subjective genitive. The word "sanctification" is a noun of action, and the word "Spirit" is in what is called "the genitive case." The word "Spirit" bears the same relationship to the word "sanctification" as the subject of a sentence does to the verb. The person or thing designated as the subject produces the action spoken of in the verb. Thus, the Holy Spirit is the one who does the sanctifying, the setting apart.

This setting apart work of the Spirit is "unto obedience," that is, it results in the obedience of the sinner to the Faith. We have the expression in Acts 6:7, "a great company of the priests were obedient to the faith." This obedience in I Peter 1:2 is not that engendered in the heart of the saint, but produced in the heart of the sinner, for it is followed by the work of God the Son in cleansing that sinner in response to his obedience. We have here the divine order; God the Father elects the sinner to salvation, God the Spirit brings him to the act of faith, and God the Son cleanses him from sin. We have the same truth brought out in II Thessalonians 2:13, "God from the beginning chose you for salvation in the sphere of the sanctification of the Spirit and in the sphere of belief of the truth." Peter's words are similar, "Peter, an ambassador of Jesus Christ with a commission to selected out ones, . . . selected out by the foreordination of God the Father to be recipients of the setting-apart work of the Spirit which results in obedience (of faith) and sprinkling of the blood of Jesus Christ."[1] This is the pre-salvation work of the Holy Spirit in which He takes up His work of bringing the sinner chosen before the foundation of the universe to the act of faith in the Lord Jesus.

An instance of the pre-salvation work of the Holy Spirit is found in John 16:8, where our Lord speaks of the Holy Spirit reproving the world. The Greek word here refers to a rebuke which results in the person's confession of his guilt, or if not his confession, his conviction of sin.[2] This He does through the Word of God. This acknowledgment however on the part of the sinner is not the same as the act of placing faith in the Lord Jesus for salvation. It is the result of one of the ministries of the Holy Spirit to the unsaved, and as such leads that person on towards the place where he exercises saving faith. The Holy Spirit brings this person to new convictions concerning sin, righteousness, and judgment. The word "of" is the translation of a Greek word meaning "concerning." He comes to see under the Holy Spirit's illumination that his unbelief is sin, that the exaltation of the Lord Jesus is a proof of His righteousness, and therefore he cherishes new convictions concerning righteousness. And, seeing the distinction between sin and righteousness, he is

---

1. *Bypaths*, pp. 39-43.
2. *Treasures*, pp. 70-72.

able to understand that the world's rejection of Christ as seen at the Cross is the same as his rejection of Christ, and that if he persists in that rejection, he will share in the judgment that was meted out to the "prince of this world," namely, Satan.

In Hebrews 6:4-6, we have more of the pre-salvation work of the Spirit. Through the Word, He enlightens the unsaved, and enables them to have a certain appreciation of the blessedness that salvation brings to the one who receives Christ as Saviour. As the recipient of these ministries of the Spirit, this unsaved person is said to be a partaker of the Holy Ghost. The word "partaker" is the translation of a Greek word that literally means "one who holds with another." It is translated "partner" in Luke 5:7. It does not imply that this person possesses the Holy Spirit as an indweller, but merely that he has willingly co-operated with Him in allowing Him to lead him on toward Christ. A further work of the Spirit for the unsaved is to produce repentance in his mind and heart. The word "repentance" is the translation of a Greek word which means in the verb, "to change one's mind," and in the noun, "a change of mind." When the Spirit reproves the unsaved concerning sin, He causes that one to change his mind regarding it. Before, he loved it. Now, he turns against it and desires the Lord Jesus to break its power in his life. He desires to be done with it. He changes his mind regarding righteousness. Before, he hated it. Now, he wants it in his life. He changes his mind regarding judgment in that, instead of remaining under the wrath of God, he takes refuge in His grace. The final step in the Spirit's ministry to this unsaved person as He leads him on to Christ is to impart to him the necessary faith to appropriate the Lord Jesus as Saviour. There is nothing in the totally depraved sin-darkened heart of the unsaved that would cause him to turn to the Saviour, turn away from his sin, and desire holiness. The hand of faith must be motivated by the Spirit. In Ephesians 2:8 we have, "By grace are ye saved through faith; and that not of yourselves: it is the gift of God." The word "that" cannot in the Greek be made to refer to "faith." It is in the neuter

gender whereas the word "faith" is in the feminine gender. It refers
to the general idea of salvation in the context. The meaning is that
we are saved by grace, and that salvation does not find its source
in us. That salvation is the gift of God. But the fact that faith is
embedded in this statement, makes it clear that it is included in
the salvation which God provides.

This pre-salvation work of the Spirit is spoken of in Scripture
as the sanctification of the Spirit. It is the setting-apart work of
the Spirit in that He sets the unsaved person apart from his unbelief
to the act of faith, from his standing in the first Adam which brought
him sin and death, to a new standing in the Last Adam which brings
him righteousness and life. This we call positional sanctification.

We come now to progressive sanctification. This is spoken of in
I Thessalonians 5:23, "And the very God of peace sanctify you
wholly; and I pray God your whole spirit and soul and body be
preserved blameless unto the coming of our Lord Jesus Christ."
Literally it is, "And the God of peace set you apart wholly." This
refers to the work of the Holy Spirit setting the believer apart from
sin, which is His work of putting sin out of the believer's life and
keeping it out as that believer trusts Him to do that for him, and
His work of setting the believer apart to a holy life, which is His
work of producing His own fruit in the believer's life as the believer
trusts Him to do that for him. These two aspects of the Spirit's
work for the believer will be taken up more fully under the heading,
"The Fullness of the Spirit."

The Fellowship and Communion of the Spirit

In Philippians 2:2, Paul exhorts the saints to be likeminded, to
have the same love, to be of one accord, of one mind. In verse one
he gives the reasons why such unity is expected of the saints, and
why it should naturally obtain. One of these is that there is "a
certain fellowship of the Spirit." In II Corinthians 13:14 we have
the apostolic benediction, "the grace of the Lord Jesus Christ, and

the love of God, and the communion of the Holy Ghost, be with
you all. Amen." The question before us is, "What is meant by the
fellowship and communion of the Holy Ghost?"

We will put aside the two English words and proceed to solid
ground, the Greek text. Too often we interpret the Bible by putting
upon certain English words a meaning which is current usage with
us in our ordinary conversation, and we do that without even consulting a dictionary. The two words "fellowship" and "communion,"
are the translation of one Greek word which we will carefully study.
Moulton and Milligan in their *Vocabulary of the Greek Testament*
cite the following examples of its use in secular documents: It is
used in a marriage contract of the time of Augustus, in the phrase
"to a *joint-participation in* the necessaries of life;" "*Belonging in
common to;*" "My brother on my father's side with whom I have no
partnership." They quote the phrase, "aiming to have *fellowship*
with Zeus" as comparable with I John 1:6 "If we say that we have
fellowship with him, and walk in darkness, we lie, and do not the
truth." Zeus was the principal god of the Greeks.

Thayer in his *Greek-English Lexicon of the New Testament* gives
the following on this word; "association, community, joint-participation, intercourse, the share which one has in anything, participation."
Commenting on I John 1:3, 6 he says, "which fellowship consists in
the fact that Christians are partakers in common of the same mind
as God and Christ, and of the blessings arising therefrom."

Our next task will be to examine every place where this Greek
word is found in the New Testament and where it is translated by
the words "fellowship" and "communion," and look at its usage.
Paul thanks God for the fellowship of the Philippian saints in the
Gospel, namely, their joint-participation with him in the progress
of the Gospel (Phil. 1:3-5).[1] In Ephesians 3:1-12 he speaks of a
mystery which was hid in God's heart until it was revealed to Paul,
and through Paul was given to the Church. It was given him "to

---

1. *Treasures*, pp. 55, 56.

make all men see what is the fellowship of this mystery." That is, the mystery is not known only to God now, but He is sharing it with believers, the word "sharing" expressing what the word "fellowship" here means. In Philippians 3:7-10, Paul has suffered the loss of all things that he may know the fellowship of Christ's sufferings, that is, be associated with Christ in His sufferings, have joint-participation with Him in those sufferings.

In I John 1:3, the apostle writes to the Christians in the Church at large, that he has in his Gospel reported the things which he heard Jesus say and which he saw Jesus do, and this, in order that they might have fellowship with him, namely joint-participation with John in the knowledge of the things Jesus said and did. That is, John tells them that he wishes to share these things with them. When he says, "Truly, our fellowship is with the Father, and with his Son Jesus Christ," we repeat Thayer's words, "which fellowship consists in the fact that Christians are partakers in common of the same mind as God and Christ, and of the blessings arising therefrom." God and His child have things in common. Then "if we (who profess to be Christians) say that we have fellowship with him (have things in common with Him), and walk in darkness, we lie, and do not the truth" (I John 1:6). That is, the things possessed in common here are a like nature, and thus the same likes and dislikes. But to be a partaker of the divine nature, to love holiness and hate sin, makes impossible a life lived in the darkness of sin. "But if we walk in the light as he is in the light, we (God and the believer) have fellowship one with another." The thing possessed in common here by both God and the saint is light. In the case of God, He is as to His essence, light. In the case of the believer, he lives in the sphere of the light which God is (I John 1:7).

Paul says in I Corinthians 1:9, "God is faithful, by whom ye were called unto the fellowship of his Son Jesus Christ our Lord." The words "fellowship of his Son" do not here mean "a communion or partnership with His Son." It is the possessive genitive here, namely, "into a communion or joint-participation belonging to His

Son, and named after His Son, and of which He is the Founder"
(*Expositor's Greek Testament*). The Greek word here denotes a
collective participation. In this the saints partake "with all those
that call on the name of the Lord Jesus." This fellowship is a
sharing in common on the part of all the saints. Its content, namely,
that which all the saints share in, is sonship to God, for it is a communion of His Son, and this is with Christ, since He is the "first-
born among many brethren," and heirship with Christ, for the
saints are joint-heirs with Christ.

In Acts 2:42 we have, "And they continued steadfastly in the
apostle's doctrine and fellowship, and in breaking of bread, and
in prayers." Vincent comments on this verse by saying that the
Greek word we are considering refers to "a relation between individuals which involves a common interest and a mutual, active
participation in that interest and in each other." In Galatians 2:9
we have, "And when James, Cephas, and John, who seemed to be
pillars, perceived the grace that was given unto me, they gave to me
and Barnabas the right hand of fellowship; that we should go
unto the heathen, and they unto the circumcision." The word "fellowship" here refers to the common interest which all had in the
salvation of the lost, and a mutual, active participation in that
interest.

The Macedonian churches had given a liberal gift of money to
Paul for needy saints, and the apostle says, "Praying us with much
intreaty that we would receive the gift and take upon us the fellowship of the ministering to the saints" (II Cor. 8:4). Here the Macedonian Christians who gave the money for the saints, ask Paul to
become their partner in its distribution. Thus we have the idea of
sharing, a sharing in the work of supplying needy saints with money,
the Macedonians, the givers, Paul, the distributor.

We will now look at the passages where the word "communion"
is the translation of our Greek word. In I Corinthians 10:16 we
have, "The cup of blessing which we bless, is it not the communion

of the blood of Christ? The bread which we break, is it not the communion of the body of Christ?" *Expositor's Greek Testament* has this to say: "The Lord's Supper constitutes a 'communion' centering in Christ, as the Jewish festal rites centered in 'the altar,' and as 'the demons,' the unseen objects of idolatrous worship, supply their basis of communion in idolatrous feasts. Such fellowship involves (1) *the ground of communion,* the sacred object celebrated in common; (2) *the association* established amongst celebrants, separating them from all others: The word 'communion' denotes the fellowship of persons with persons in one and the same object." Thus, in the Lord's Supper, believers participate together in Christ, in the recognition of His atonement on their behalf, and in remembrance of His death until He comes.

In II Corinthians 6:14 we have, "What communion hath light with darkness?" One could translate, "What things does light have in common with darkness?" Is there any common interest or mutual activity in which they participate one with another?

We are now ready to consider the meaning of the words, "fellowship of the Spirit," and "communion of the Holy Ghost," in the light of the study which we have just made of the Greek word which is translated by the words "fellowship" and "communion." The word "Ghost" is the translation of the same Greek word which is in other places rendered "Spirit." The Greek word, we have found, has the following meanings; "joint-participation, belonging in common to, a partnership, association, intercourse, sharing, a relation between individuals which involves a common interest and a mutual, active participation in that interest and in each other."

Therefore, when Paul speaks of a certain fellowship of the Holy Spirit that obtains in the lives of the saints, he refers to that relationship between the Spirit and the saint which involves a common interest and a mutual, active participation in that interest. That is, as the result of the Spirit's work in regeneration and in His control over the saint as the saint is definitely subjected to Him, there has been brought about in the life of the saint, a joint-participation on the part of the believer with the Holy Spirit in an interest and a mutual and active participation in the things of God and the work of God in saving lost souls. It is a partnership, so to speak, between God and the believer. Paul speaks of this in the words, "We are laborers together with God" (I Cor. 3:9). Another interest held in common is the Christian life and testimony of the believer. The Holy Spirit is desirous of producing the highest type of Christian experience in the life of the believer, and the believer has the same interest, and shows it by maintaining an attitude of dependence upon and trust in the Holy Spirit to produce that life in him. This fellowship is a co-operation on the part of the saint with the Holy Spirit in His work of sanctification. When Paul in his apostolic benediction prays that the communion of the Holy Ghost be with all the saints, he is asking that this mutual interest and activity may continue and become more rich and effective in the lives of the saints.

We now come to a consideration of the English word "fellowship." In its current usage among the saints, it refers to the fellowship which saints have with one another, that is, the companionship and friendliness and sociability which is enjoyed when the saints get together in prayer-meeting or preaching service, or in other Christian society. Hence, there is a danger of thinking that the phrase "fellowship of the Spirit" means "companionship with the Spirit." Right here is where some leave the path of sound doctrine and practice. They seek the Holy Spirit and His fullness for His sake alone. They seek intercourse with Him as an end in itself. Thus they lay themselves open to the snares of Satan and the control of evil spirits. There is no such thing in Scripture as the believer's fellowship or companionship with the Spirit comparable to the believer's fellowship or companionship with the Lord Jesus. The Holy Spirit's ministry is to glorify the Son, and in doing that He always calls the believer's attention to the Lord Jesus, never to Himself. He keeps Himself in the background. The Lord Jesus

must always be central in the life of the saint. He is the One with
whom we have fellowship in the commonly accepted usage of the
word today. The Holy Spirit makes this possible. Sir Robert Ander-
son's words are to the point here: "In proportion therefore as mind
and heart are fixed on Christ, we may count on the Spirit's presence
and power, but if we make the Holy Ghost Himself the object of our
aspirations and worship, some false spirit may counterfeit the true
and take us for a prey."

The association which the correctly instructed saint has with the
Holy Spirit, is in the form of a moment-by-moment conscious dependence upon Him, a trust in Him for His guidance and strength, and a
yielding to Him for His ministry of putting sin out of the life and
keeping it out, and of radiating the beauty of the Lord Jesus through
his every thought, word, and deed, this, together with a co-operation
with Him which takes the form of a mutual interest and active
participation in the things of God.

G. D. Watson in *Living Words* has put this very beautifully in
the following words: "The Holy Spirit will put a strict watch over
you with a jealous love, and will rebuke you for little words and
feelings, or for wasting your time, which other Christians never
seem distressed over. So make up your mind that God is an infinite
Sovereign, and has a right to do as He pleases with His own. He
may not explain to you a thousand things which puzzle your reason
in His dealings with you, but if you absolutely sell yourself to be
His love slave, He will wrap you up in a jealous love, and bestow
upon you many blessings which come only to those who are in the
inner circle.

"Settle it forever, then, that you are to deal directly with the Holy
Spirit, and that He is to have the privilege of tying your tongue, or
chaining your hand, or closing your eyes, in ways that He does not
seem to use with others. Now when you are so possessed with the
living God that you are, in your secret heart, pleased and delighted
over this peculiar, personal, private, jealous guardianship and man-

agement of the Holy Spirit over your life, you will have found the vestibule of heaven."

The Fullness of the Spirit

Our first task will be to inquire as to the exact meaning of the word "fullness" when used in connection with the ministry of the Spirit. The phrases, "filled with the Holy Spirit" and "full of the Holy Spirit," are used in the Authorized Version. They are the translation of either one of two verbs and of a noun. The verb *pimplemi* is used in Luke 1:15, 41, 67; Acts 2:4, 4:8, 31, 13:9. An illustration of its use other than with the word "Spirit" is in the phrase, "were filled with fear" (Luke 5:26). Thayer in his Greek-English lexicon has this to say about the use of this verb here: "What wholly takes possession of the mind, is said to fill it." Thus, the expression, "filled with the Holy Spirit" speaks of the Spirit possessing the mind and heart of the believer. This possession implies His control over that mind and heart. Thus the words "full" and "filled" refer to the control which the Spirit exerts over the believer who is said to be filled with Him.

The other verb is *pleroo*, and is used in Acts 13:52 and Ephesians 5:18. An example of its use other than that in relation to the Spirit is in the sentence, "Sorrow hath filled your heart" (John 16:6). Thayer says of its usage here, "to pervade, take possession of." Thus, as sorrow possessed or controlled the hearts of the disciples, so the Holy Spirit possesses or controls the believer who is said to be filled with Him.

The noun *pleres* is used in Luke 4:1; Acts 6:3, 5, 7:55, 9:17, 11:24. In Acts 6:5 it is used in the phrase "full of faith." Thayer says of this use, "thoroughly permeated Stephen in the sense that it possessed or controlled him." Thus, the fullness of the Holy Spirit refers to His control over the believer who is said to be filled with Him.

But let us press the point still further by looking at the Greek grammar involved in these expressions. In the expression, "filled with the Holy Spirit," we have the verb "filled" in the passive voice, the subject in this case being inactive and being acted upon by an outside agent, and the noun "Spirit" in the genitive case, the genitive of description, indicating what the "filling" consisted of. The "filling" in this case refers to a certain control exerted over the believer. The word "Spirit" thus indicates who is exerting this control. The expression "full of the Holy Spirit" is from a noun "full," and another noun "Spirit," the latter in the genitive case. The noun "full," meaning here "control," is a noun of action. We have here a Greek construction called the subjective genitive, in which the noun in the genitive case, here "Spirit," produces the action in the noun of action, "full." Thus, the Holy Spirit is the One who exerts control over the believer said to be filled with Him.

There is just one instance in the New Testament where the words "filled with the Spirit" are not followed by the genitive case. In Ephesians 5:18 we have the verb followed by the instrumental case, which latter case designates that by means of which the action in the verb is performed. The action in the verb here is a certain control exerted over the believer. The Holy Spirit is the divine instrument who exerts this control. One could translate, "Be controlled by the Spirit."

We must not think of the Holy Spirit filling our hearts as water fills a bottle, or air, a vacuum, or a bushel of oats, an empty basket. The heart of a Christian is not a receptacle to be emptied in order that the Holy Spirit might fill it. The Holy Spirit is not a substance to fill an empty receptacle. He is a Person to control another person, the believer. He does not fill a Christian's life with Himself. He controls that person.

The heart is a symbol used to refer to the will, the reason, and the emotions. Thus, the Holy Spirit possesses or controls the volitional, rational, and emotional activities of the believer who is said to be filled with Him. He brings all these into the place of obedience and conformity to the Word of God. Therefore, when we speak of a Christian filled with the Spirit, we are referring to the control which a divine Person, the Holy Spirit, has over a human being, the believer.

The believer is exhorted, "Be filled with the Spirit" (Eph. 5:18), or as we have translated it, "Be controlled by the Spirit." The tendency of the unsaved person is seen in the words of the hymn, "I was a wandering sheep, I did not love the fold, I did not love my Shepherd's voice, I would not be controlled." This tendency is broken when a sinner is saved, in that God breaks the power of the sinful nature, which nature had exerted absolute control over him, and gives him His own divine nature. The believer is then exhorted to be controlled by the Holy Spirit. The Holy Spirit's ministry in the premises is to maintain in the actual experience of the Christian, that which God did for him the moment He saved him. The Holy Spirit suppresses the activities of the evil nature whose power was broken, and produces His fruit in the life. The very fact that an individual is exhorted to do something, demands as a logical accompaniment, that person's exercise of his will in the doing of that thing. That is, the believer here is not automatically controlled by the Spirit just because the Spirit indwells him. The control which the Spirit exerts over the believer is dependent upon the believer's active and correct adjustment to the Spirit. The Lord Jesus did not save us until we recognized Him as the Saviour and put our trust in Him for salvation. Just so, the Holy Spirit does not control us in the sense of permeating our will, reason, and emotions, until we recognize Him as the One who has been sent by the Father to sanctify our lives, and trust Him to perform His ministry in and through us. There must be an ever present conscious dependence upon and definite subjection to the Holy Spirit, a constant yielding to His ministry and leaning upon Him for guidance and power, if He is to control the believer *in the most efficient manner and with the largest and best results.* The Lord Jesus waited for you and me to recognize Him as Saviour before He saved us. The Holy Spirit indwelling a believer is waiting to be recognized as the One to come to that believer's aid. Salvation is by faith from start to finish. It is a work of God for man. But God waits for man, unsaved or saved as the case might be, to avail himself of the salvation he needs, by means of faith. One of the reasons why the Holy Spirit has so little control over many Christians is because they think He works automatically in their hearts.

Our Lord in John 7:37, 38 lays down two simple requirements for the fullness of the Spirit, a thirst for His control and a trust in the Lord Jesus for the Spirit's control.

"If any man thirst" refers to a desire on the part of the believer that the Holy Spirit be the One to control his every thought, word, and deed. We do not take a drink of water unless we are thirsty. We do not appropriate the control of the Spirit unless we desire Him to control us. A desire for His control will include among other things, a desire that He cause us to judge sin in our lives, a desire that He put sin out of our lives and keep it out, a desire that He separate us from all the ties we might have with that system of evil called the world, a desire that He dethrone our self-life and enthrone the Lord Jesus as absolute Lord and Master, a desire that He produce in us His own fruit, a desire that He make us Christlike, a desire that He lead us and teach us. Such a desire is a serious thing. It involves crucifixion of self, and self dies hard. The Spirit-controlled life is a crucified life. The other requirement is trust. Our Lord said, "He that believeth on Me, out from his inmost being shall flow rivers of living water." The trust here in this context is not only trust in Him as Saviour, but trust in Him as the One who fills with the Spirit. *The Spirit-controlled life is a matter of trust.* Salvation is by faith. We received our justification by faith. We are to receive our sanctification by faith. It is this constant desire for the Spirit's control and a trust in the Lord Jesus for the Spirit's control that results in the Spirit-controlled life. When one faces a new day, it is well to include in our prayers thanksgiving for the presence of the Holy Spirit in our hearts, the expression of our desire for His control, and a definite assertion of our trust in the Lord Jesus for the Spirit's control during that day. It is well at intervals during the day when we are faced with temptation, or when we have a definite piece of Christian service to perform, or are in need of instruction from the Word or of strength for some duty, to recognize quietly the ministry of the Spirit and depend upon Him for all needed guidance, wisdom, and strength. He is waiting for us to recognize Him and trust Him for His aid. He is there, the indwelling Spirit, always at the service of the believer. But the point is that He comes to our aid when we avail ourselves of His help. There are just two things therefore which the believer must do in order to be controlled by the Spirit, desire that control and trust the Lord Jesus for that control.

There is no Scripture for the practice of asking for the fullness of the Spirit for one's self. Our Lord in Luke 11:13 said to His disciples, "How much more shall your heavenly Father give the Holy Spirit to them that ask Him?" He invited the disciples to ask for the Person of the Spirit, not His fullness. This was before Pentecost, and the Spirit had not yet come. It appears that they did not ask the Father for Him, and so our Lord says "I will pray the Father, and he shall give you another Comforter" (John 14:16). The "I" is intensive. They had not asked, so He did. The result was Pentecost. Distinguish therefore between asking for the Person of the Holy Spirit and for His fullness or control. It is not maintained that a believer who asks for the fullness of the Spirit does not experience His control over his life. Sometimes he does and sometimes he does not. If he asks in faith believing and at the same time yields his whole life to His control, and desires to be done with sin, the control of the Spirit follows. *But too often such asking is accompanied by an unyielded life.* But a trust in the Lord Jesus for that control involves the heart's submission to the Spirit. It involves the entire moral and spiritual being of the Christian. Many a sinner fearing the dire consequences of sin, has asked the Lord Jesus to save him, but has not been willing to give up his sin. Many a saint has asked the Holy Spirit to fill him, desiring more power for service, but has been unwilling to make a clean sweep of things and be done with some little pet sin in his life. But a statement of trust in the Lord Jesus for that fullness, forces one to face the sin question and the lack of surrender, and to be done with both. Furthermore, asking for that control may not be accompanied by trust but unbelief. A simple, "Lord Jesus, I do desire that the Holy Spirit control my every thought, word, and deed, and I do trust Thee for that control of the Spirit over my life," is the scriptural way of appropriating the fullness of the Spirit. If one is disposed to say, "Why split hairs and be so technical about this," one could cite the exactness with which our Lord uses His words in reference to the Holy Spirit when He says, "For he dwelleth with you and shall be in you" (John 14:17), thus distinguishing between the presence of the Spirit *with* the believer in Old Testament times under the law, and the presence of the Spirit *in* the believer under grace.

There is no Scripture for the practice of tarrying for the fullness of the Spirit. Our Lord said to the disciples, "I send the promise of my Father upon you: but tarry ye in the city of Jerusalem until ye be endued with power from on high" (Luke 24:49). But let us note some careful distinctions here. He did not tell them to tarry for the fullness, but for the Person and the coming of the Spirit. The Holy Spirit was scheduled to come to earth fifty days after the resurrection, as Pentecost was fifty days after the Feast of First Fruits. The disciples were to wait in Jerusalem for ten more days, and the Spirit would come. This announcement by our Lord was made at the close of His forty day post-resurrection ministry. The Holy Spirit came at Pentecost. The word "tarry" is the translation of a Greek word that means "to sit down, to sojourn." They were to sojourn in the city of Jerusalem for ten days until the Holy Spirit came from heaven. He is here. We need not wait for Him. He indwells the believer the moment that person puts his faith in the Lord Jesus, and He awaits that person's desire and trust that He control him.

One may be disposed to quote Acts 19:2, "Have ye received the Holy Ghost since ye believed?" arguing that the Holy Spirit does not come in to abide until the child of God has come to a certain stage in his Christian experience. But the correct rendering is, "Did ye receive the Spirit when ye believed?" Paul was surprised at the absence of spirituality in these believers. It turned out that they had followed the preaching of John the Baptist, and therefore had not come under the provision of the indwelling Spirit of the Age of Grace.[1]

Or, one might say, "I am a Christian, but I do not have the Holy Spirit because I do not speak in tongues," quoting Acts 2:4, 10:46, and 19:6. But let us be careful to note that Acts 2:4 refers to the languages of the individuals mentioned in Acts 2:8-11, that the speaking in tongues of Acts 10:46 was an evidence for that time given to the Jews, that the Gentiles had also received the Spirit, the need for which is now past, and that Acts 19:6 has to do with a special case where Jews had come into salvation under the Old Testament dispensation of law and now were receiving the added benefits of the Age of Grace, a case which cannot occur today.

But again, one may insist that a believer does not receive the Spirit except by the laying on of hands, quoting Acts 8:17 and 19:6. The act of laying on of hands always signifies identification. In the case of Acts 8:17, the Samaritans who did not recognize the temple at Jerusalem, needed to recognize the authority of the church at that place. Submission to the laying on of the apostles' hands thus healed the breach between those Samaritans and the Christian Jews, and identified the former with the Jerusalem church. In Acts 19:6 we have Jews coming over into a new dispensation and authority, and a similar situation holds true for them. We have no such conditions today, and therefore the laying on of hands is not needed for the reception of the Spirit. Thus a consciousness of the

---

1. *Nuggets,* pp. 96, 97.

personal presence of the Holy Spirit in the believer, a desire for His control, and a trust in the Lord Jesus for that control, is the scriptural way of appropriating the ministry of the Holy Spirit.

This condition of being filled with the Spirit must not be a spasmodic thing in the life of the Christian. One hears teaching to the effect that the Holy Spirit fills one only when he is engaged in some particular piece of Christian service. That idea comes from the Old Testament ministry of the Holy Spirit. Before Pentecost, He came upon believers in order to equip them for a certain work they were to do for God, and left them when that service was over. But in the Church Age, this procedure does not obtain. The command, "Be filled (controlled) with the Spirit" is in a grammatical construction in Greek which speaks of a continuous process or state, as the case might be. For those who know Greek, we might say that the imperative mode in the aorist tense speaks of the fact of an action, while that mode in the present tense speaks of a continuous process or state. Here we have the present imperative. The tense in Greek used when a writer speaks of the fact of an action, is the aorist. When he uses any other tense, he goes out of his way to do so, and for the purpose of adding details. Had the inspired writer used the aorist tense here, he would have referred to the fact of being filled with the Spirit. But since he uses the present tense, he desires his Greek reader to understand that the exhortation is for one to be constantly, moment by moment, filled with the Spirit. That is, God's plan for the normal Christian life is that it should be a life constantly, consciously, and definitely subjected to the Spirit, a life that has a consuming desire for His control over every thought, word, and deed, thus a life unceasingly controlled by the Holy Spirit. The Christian needs this constant control of the Spirit over his life if he is to gain constant victory over sin, if the Lord Jesus in His beauty and fragrance of character is to be radiated by the Spirit through the life of the saint, if the saint is to walk in the path of God's will for him, if he is to live a life of prayer, and if he expects to understand his Bible as he should. *One cannot do with less than the Spirit's constant control.* Indeed, it is a sin not to be filled constantly with the Spirit. The mode of the verb is imperative. That means, that the words "Be filled" are a command. Failure to obey any command of Scripture is sin.

One hears the expression, "One baptism, many fillings." The first half of this expression is correct, but the second half is not in accord with the scriptural ideal for a normal Christian life. Let us look at the words, "many fillings." They speak of the Spirit-filled life as one would speak of a motor-car and its need of gasoline. That is, the filling-station attendant fills the tank. We drive off. The running motor consumes the gasoline and the tank becomes empty, and must be filled again. This is the illustration of the believer who is filled with the Spirit, engages in a piece of Christian work, lives through certain experiences, and in doing so, uses up the power which came from that filling with the Spirit. Then he must come back to the Spirit for another supply of power. This process is repeated over and over again.

But the thing wrong with all this is that the Christian's heart is not an empty receptacle to be filled with a substance as the tank of a motor car is to be filled with gasoline, but is a symbol of the will, the emotions, and the reason, all of which are to be constantly controlled. Again, the Spirit is not a certain amount of power given to the believer which he can use in his activities. He is a Person who controls another person, the believer. It is not that the believer uses the power of God but that God's power uses him. Furthermore, the only things that would deprive the Christian of this fullness of the Spirit are a lack of definite subjection on his part to the Spirit, or the presence of known and cherished sin in his life. Instead of saying, "One baptism, and many fillings," one should say, "One baptism, and His constant control."

But this desire for the control of the Holy Spirit, and this trust in the Lord Jesus for that control, is but part of the believer's obligation in the premises. One cannot say, "Just to realize with joy the Spirit's passionate longing to control my thoughts, words, and deeds for the glory of the Lord Jesus, and to rest quietly in His energizing and supervising ministry, is all that is necessary." *The Christian life is not a mere "let go and let God" affair. It is a "take hold with God" business.* It is not a mere rest in God, an existence somewhat like that of a jelly-fish floating in the warm currents of the Gulf Stream. God is not developing jelly-fish Christians. God wants to develop heroes, Christian men and women of moral stamina and spiritual power. In the physical realm, no one becomes strong by merely eating wholesome food and resting. Exercise is what is needed to change the food-energy into bone and muscle. In like manner, the Christian must exercise himself spiritually if he is to grow strong in his Christian life. That demands the exercise of his free will, the making of choices, the deciding between right and wrong, the saying of a point blank NO to temptation, the constant striving to improve one's spiritual life, grow in the Christian graces and in Christlikeness. It involves not only the desire to be loving, but the definite endeavor to be loving. It is not merely a trustful rest in the Holy Spirit to make us loving, but a positive exertion of our own will to be loving. It is like bending one's arm. The strength to bend one's arm is in that member of the body, but the strength is only potential and not active unless the will power is exerted which will cause that strength to function. Just so, the power of the Holy Spirit is potentially resident in the saint by virtue of His indwelling presence, but it is only operative in that believer when he is yielded to and dependent upon the ministry of the Spirit, and then steps out in faith in the performance of the action contemplated. For instance, when the believer is confronted with a temptation, it is not enough to rest in the Holy Spirit's ministry to overcome that temptation for us. We must by an act of our own free will say a bold, positive, and fearless NO to it. The instant we move in that direction, the Spirit is there with His wonderful energizing power. Indeed, you will say, that the very start of the step taken in the direction of the act of saying NO to that temptation was motivated by the Spirit. And that is true. Yet it is also true that it is the free action of the believer's will, and is his responsibility. Right here lies that mysterious, incomprehensible, and not-to-be-understood interaction and mutual response between the free-will of man and the sovereign grace of God.

This necessary action of the will on the part of the believer, in addition to the trust in and dependence upon the Holy Spirit which the saint must have, is seen clearly in the expression, "a certain fellowship of the Spirit" (Phil. 2:1) which we found referred to "a relation between individuals which involves a common interest and a mutual active participation in that interest and in each other." It is the obligation of the believer to be supremely interested in the things of God, for the Spirit is constantly exploring the deep things of God (I Cor. 2:10). The Christian who does not maintain a real interest in and hunger for the Word of God, and satisfy both by a constant study of that Word, is not co-operating with the Spirit, and is not giving the Spirit an opportunity to work in his life and cause him to grow in the Christian graces. The Spirit works through the Word of God that we have stored in our hearts, and not apart from it.

Likewise, the believer who does not actively participate in the activity necessary to the saying of YES to the will of God and of NO to sin, is not co-operating with the Spirit. And the Christian who does not engage in a Holy Spirit directed ministry of some kind in the work of furthering the knowledge of the Word of God, is not co-operating with the Spirit. It is this ideal combination of a moment by moment trust in, submission to, and dependence upon the ministry of the Holy Spirit, and the constant interest in and participation with the Holy Spirit in the things of God, that produces the best results in the Christian's experience. This combination develops Christian men and women with a sense of responsibility, with moral courage and stamina of a high order, with a balance and poise that weathers the severest storms, with a delicate sense of tact that enables them to move among their fellowmen without riding roughshod over their tender hearts, but rather in a loving way so that their passing leaves a sense of the presence of the Lord Jesus. It develops spiritual giants, men and women who can be trusted in a time of crisis.

Inaccurate Statements

It seems rather singular that the only branch of Christian doctrine in which we allow ourselves a certain looseness and inaccuracy of statement is in regard to the Person and work of the Holy Spirit. The plea is, "Why be so technical? We all mean the same thing, even though we may use different terms or expressions to convey our thoughts." But do we allow ourselves a like looseness and inaccuracy of statement when we speak of the Person and work of the Lord Jesus? How carefully we guard the doctrine of His virgin birth, and His deity, making a careful distinction between His divinity and deity.[1] How meticulous we are in our choice of words when we formulate the doctrine of His substitutionary death on the Cross. We distinguish between His coming into the air to catch out the Church and His coming to the earth to set up the Millennial Kingdom. To be just a bit inaccurate in a statement regarding the origin of our Lord's humanity, the meaning of His death on the Cross, and the fact of His bodily resurrection, would brand one as a heretic, in present day language, a Modernist. But to play fast and loose with the plainly revealed truth regarding the Person and work of the Holy Spirit, produces no protest in evangelical circles.

If an evangelist would be as inaccurate in his statements regarding the need of a lost sinner for a Saviour, the work of that Saviour on the Cross, and the way a sinner must appropriate that salvation, as we allow ourselves to be when we teach the saints about the ministry of the Spirit, how many souls would be saved? It is the clear, simple, accurate, true to the Word statements of the evangelist which the Holy Spirit uses. And if lost souls would be kept from

---

1. *Treasures*, pp. 74-76.

salvation by a message which does not accurately explain the way
of salvation, then saints are being deprived of the most efficient
ministry of the Holy Spirit because of the obscurities and inaccura-
cies so prevalent in much of the teaching regarding His Person and
work.   One of the chief reasons for the lack of power in the
Church is that the Holy Spirit is not recognized as He should be
by the individual Christian. And much of this lack of understanding
of the ministry of the Spirit on the part of the saint is due to the
inaccurate presentation of that important truth. Such a presentation
not only misinforms but makes it harder, sometimes well-nigh impossible for the clear, simple truth to be taught successfully.

Two of the most serious and harmful of these loose and inaccurate
statements are petitions addressed to the Spirit in which the believer
asks Him to fall fresh upon him, and to descend upon his heart.
Two of the plainest truths in Scripture are the coming of the Spirit
at Pentecost to form the Church, and His coming into the heart
of the believer at the moment he receives the Lord Jesus as his
Saviour, to take up His permanent residence in his being. To voice
such petitions as those above, is to ignore and deny the plain teaching of Scripture. It is to give the believer the impression that the
Holy Spirit is a far away Helper who does not dwell permanently
in the heart of the saint, but comes to his aid when he calls. Thus,
the believer does not have the consciousness of the indwelling Spirit.
He does not see that his body is an inner sanctuary in which the
Holy Spirit dwells. It is to ask for a second Pentecost. It is to
ask for the coming of the Person of the Spirit when what the saint
needs and possibly desires is the fullness of the Spirit. In that case,
where is the proper adjustment of the believer to the Spirit which
would enable Him to exercise His most efficient control over him?
How senseless to meet a friend, have that friend at one's side, and
yet plead with him to come to one. What would this friend think
of us? And what does the Holy Spirit think of such looseness in
presenting the proper relationship of the Spirit to the believer?
The fellowship of two human beings with one another is the most

delicate and intricate of all relationships, demanding the most perfect mutual adjustment to and understanding of one another if that fellowship is to be of a high order. The same thing is true of the fellowship of the Spirit with respect to the believer. And if the proper adjustment is not made on the part of the saint, then the Spirit is prevented from performing His ministry in and for that saint in an efficient way. When a believer is taught to ask the Spirit to fall fresh on him and to descend upon his heart, he is taught to ignore the truth concerning His indwelling. Furthermore, the idea of the descending Spirit falling fresh upon him takes the place of the conception of the fullness or control of the Spirit over his life, and the believer does not put himself into His control. The result is that the Spirit is prevented from doing His best for the believer, and the saint lives a powerless mediocre Christian life.

Another wrong conception concerning the adjustment of the believer to the Holy Spirit is found in the idea that the believer must empty his heart of sin and self and live a separated life in order that the Holy Spirit can fill his heart. This is based again upon the misapprehension that the Christian's heart is a receptacle, and the Spirit a substance to fill the space otherwise unoccupied. The word "heart" as used here is just a figure of speech which speaks of the will, emotions, and reason of the individual, and the Holy Spirit is a divine Person who seeks to control and use these to the glory of God.

This puts the cart before the horse. A Christian who attempts to clean up his life by ridding his life of all sin, in order that he may be filled with the Spirit, will never be filled with the Spirit. It is just as impossible for a *sinner* to rid his life of sin and live a life in obedience to God's Word in order to receive the Lord Jesus as Saviour, as it is for the *saint* to dethrone self and enthrone the Lord Jesus, live a separated life, and put all sin out of his life in order to be filled with the Spirit. It takes the precious blood of Jesus and the omnipotent power of God to save a sinner. It takes the omnipotent power of the Spirit to put sin out of a Christian's life, to enthrone the Lord Jesus, and to cut the saint's mooring lines with the world. The lost sinner comes to the Lord Jesus saying, "Just as I am without one plea, but that thy blood was shed for me." The saint with sin in his life should come to the Holy Spirit just as he is, with all his spiritual problems, and judging the sin in his life for what it is, namely sin, consciously exert his free will and say NO to the temptation to continue in that sin, and trust the Holy Spirit to put it out of his life and keep it out, depending upon Him to give both the desire and power to keep from committing that sin again. The Holy Spirit is eager to come to the aid of a saint who is not getting victory over sin, and make actual in his life that victory which the Lord Jesus procured for him at the Cross. It is the Holy Spirit who will clean up the believer's life as he co-operates with Him. He will enthrone the Lord Jesus as Lord of the life as the saint trusts Him to do this. He will cause the believer to live a life in separation from the world and unto God.

Then there is the practice of referring to the Holy Spirit as "it." "It" is a neuter pronoun and is used to refer to things, never persons. To use the pronoun "it" is to deny personality to that which is referred to. Observe what evils follow the practice of using this pronoun when referring to the Holy Spirit. It deprives Him of personality in the conception of the speaker and his uninformed listeners. That does away with the doctrine of His personal indwelling of the believer. That in turn takes away the practical teaching of personal holiness in view of the fact that the physical body of the believer is a temple of the Holy Spirit. Again, by denying personality to the Holy Spirit, the use of the pronoun "it" prevents the saint from bringing himself into proper adjustment to the Spirit, so that He, a Person, can control the believer. There is no heart submission to the will of the Spirit, merely the attempted appropriation of some mysterious power which the believer feels he needs and can use, which again is a wrong conception, for it is not the believer who uses the power of God but the power of God that uses him. Such a conception as that of the Holy Spirit grieving over the saint who has sin in his life, is also made impossible, and this potent check upon sin in the life of a Christian is taken away (Eph. 4:30). To sum it up; the believer who merely conceives of the Holy Spirit as an impersonal force which he can use, knows nothing either in doctrine or practice, concerning the fullness of the Spirit.

But in justification of the practice of using the neuter pronoun when referring to the Holy Spirit, some one may call attention to the fact that the Authorized Version uses the pronoun "itself" in Romans 8:16, 26, and the neuter pronoun "which," in Romans 5:5; I Corinthians 6:19; II Timothy 1:14; I Peter 1:11, and I John 3:24, when referring to the Holy Spirit. And here is where we need to go to the Greek text for an explanation which should clear up this difficulty. It will be necessary to mention some Greek grammar rules in doing this.

Nouns in Greek are in either one of three genders. They are either masculine, feminine, or neuter. They have certain endings which indicate to what gender they belong. The word "spirit" happens to be in the neuter gender. But that does not mean that the Greeks considered that which is designated by the word "spirit" as being an inanimate object and therefore impersonal. The Greek word for "wine" is masculine. But that does not mean that they ascribed personality to "wine." The Greek word "wisdom" is feminine. But that again does not mean that they thought of wisdom in a personal way. The Greek word for "child" is neuter, but they did not therefore think of a child as an inanimate thing. In English the neuter pronoun is used for inanimate objects, the masculine, for a male individual, and the feminine for the female.

Because the Greek word for "spirit" is neuter, Greek grammar requires that the pronoun used when referring to that which is designated by this Greek word, must be neuter. The translators used the neuter pronoun "itself" in Romans 8:16, 26, because the

Greek pronoun is neuter. But there is such a thing as idiom in a
language, namely, a construction or expression peculiar to that
language, and not found in other languages, which if brought over
literally into the second language, would give a wrong impression.
The business of a translator is to bring over into the second language,
the thought of the first. He is not bound to give a literal translation
of an idiom. His business is to find that expression in the second
language which will adequately translate the meaning which the
idiom has in its own language. The teaching of Scripture shows
clearly that the Holy Spirit is a Person. In view of this, the
pronoun "Himself" should be the translation in Romans 8:16, 26.
See how the personality of the Spirit is so clearly implied in the
expression, "The Spirit Himself."

The same procedure applies in the case where the word "which"
is used. In John 14:17, 26, the pronoun is in the neuter gender,
and yet the translators use the word "whom." Why did they not
follow the same procedure in the cases where they used "which?"
In all these instances the pronoun is neuter in the Greek text. They
also offer "Him" as the translation of the neuter pronoun of the
third person (John 14:17). In every instance the pronoun should
be "whom" not "which."

But again, in John 14:26, the word "he" is from a masculine pronoun in Greek. But the pronoun here is masculine because its antecedent "Comforter" is masculine. The masculine gender of this
pronoun does not teach the personality of the Spirit any more than
the pronoun in the neuter gender speaks of the Spirit as an impersonal force. The genders of the pronouns in the Greek text which
refer to the Holy Spirit are determined by the genders of their
antecedents. Suppose for a moment that the Spirit was not a
person, and that the word "spirit" was masculine. It would be
just as wrong for a translator to use the masculine pronoun "he"
if a masculine were used in the Greek, as for a translator, knowing
that the Holy Spirit is a Person, to use a neuter pronoun when a
neuter pronoun is found in the Greek text. One word for "house"

in Greek is masculine. But you would not translate its masculine pronoun by the word "he." Another word for "house" is feminine. But you would not render its feminine pronoun by the word "she." The pronoun would be "it" in both cases. The word "he" in John 16:8 is from a masculine pronoun in Greek. But that pronoun is masculine because its antecedent "Comforter" is masculine. Thus, the masculine gender of the Greek text does not teach the personality of the Spirit, nor can one therefore erroneously infer that the Spirit is not a Person but only an impersonal force just because the word "spirit" is neuter and its pronoun is therefore neuter. In every case, the English pronoun referring to the Holy Spirit should be in the masculine gender, thus showing that He is a Person, since the teaching of Scripture is that He is a Person.

INDEX

Of Scripture References Covering Volumes I to IV of This Series

The student of the English Bible often wishes that he had access to the Greek New Testament in order that he might be able to know just what Greek words are back of the English words which he is studying, and thus come to a clearer understanding of the Word. The series of books of which this one is the fourth, has been written to help meet this need. But one has more than a lexicon in them. They not only give the meaning of the Greek word, but also its particular shade of meaning and interpretation in the context in which it is found. In addition to that, these books offer a concordant study of words such as "perfect, anoint, temptation, visit, love, crown," listing the places where they are found in the New Testament, commenting on representative instances of their use, and leaving the other places for the study of the English reader. The four books treat approximately 1150 scripture references. The index to these has been placed in this fourth book for the convenience of the student. When studying a portion of the English New Testament, he can easily consult the single index and see if the author has commented upon its Greek text. The four books are: *Golden Nuggets from the Greek New Testament for the English Reader; Bypaths in the Greek New Testament for the English Reader; Treasures from the Greek New Testament for the English Reader;* and *Untranslatable Riches from the Greek New Testament for the English Reader.* These will be listed in the index under the abbreviated titles; *Nuggets, Bypaths, Treasures,* and *Riches.*

A special concordance, listing each place where the word "love" occurs in the New Testament, will be found in *Bypaths,* together with the distinctive Greek word for "love" in each instance (there are three different Greek words used), and the definition of each, with comment on representative passages. To include these in this index would make it unduly long.

INDEX

Of Scripture References Covering Volumes I to IV of This Series

SCRIPTURE	VOLUME	PAGE
Matthew 1:21	*Nuggets*	113
Matthew 2:1-8	*Bypaths*	23
Matthew 2:1-11	*Treasures*	68
Matthew 3:7	*Treasures*	86
Matthew 3:8	*Treasures*	78
Matthew 3:11	*Riches*	86
Matthew 3:11	*Treasures*	74, 76, 77
Matthew 3:16	*Treasures*	86
Matthew 4:1, 3, 7	*Treasures*	130
Matthew 4:4	*Nuggets*	120
Matthew 5:1-12	*Treasures*	20
Matthew 5:8	*Riches*	88
Matthew 5:11	*Bypaths*	76
Matthew 5:22, 29, 30	*Treasures*	44, 45
Matthew 5:43, 44	*Nuggets*	61
Matthew 5:48	*Treasures*	117
Matthew 6:2	*Treasures*	65
Matthew 6:5	*Nuggets*	62
Matthew 6:17	*Treasures*	123
Matthew 6:25	*Nuggets*	43
Matthew 7:3-5	*Nuggets*	79
Matthew 7:7, 8	*Nuggets*	87
Matthew 8:17	*Treasures*	74
Matthew 8:26	*Treasures*	72
Matthew 9:21, 22	*Bypaths*	27
Matthew 9:32	*Nuggets*	105
Matthew 10:28	*Treasures*	45
Matthew 10:37	*Nuggets*	62
Matthew 11:23	*Treasures*	46
Matthew 11:28-30	*Bypaths*	77
Matthew 12:16	*Treasures*	72
Matthew 12:22	*Treasures*	48
Matthew 12:41	*Treasures*	77
Matthew 13:3	*Nuggets*	92
Matthew 13:36	*Riches*	60
Matthew 16:1	*Treasures*	130
Matthew 16:18	*Treasures*	47
Matthew 16:18	*Nuggets*	55
Matthew 16:22	*Treasures*	72
Matthew 16:23	*Treasures*	70
Matthew 16:26	*Riches*	38
Matthew 17:2	*Nuggets*	26
Matthew 17:2	*Bypaths*	81
Matthew 17:18	*Treasures*	72

SCRIPTURE	VOLUME	PAGE
Matthew 18:8	*Treasures*	40
Matthew 18:9	*Treasures*	45
Matthew 18:15	*Treasures*	72
Matthew 19:3	*Treasures*	130
Matthew 19:13	*Treasures*	70, 72
Matthew 19:21	*Treasures*	117
Matthew 19:24	*Nuggets*	29
Matthew 20:12	*Treasures*	74
Matthew 20:28	*Treasures*	16
Matthew 20:31	*Treasures*	72
Matthew 22:15-22	*Bypaths*	22
Matthew 22:18, 35	*Treasures*	130
Matthew 23:6	*Nuggets*	62
Matthew 23:15, 33	*Treasures*	45
Matthew 23:37-39	*Treasures*	17
Matthew 25:23	*Treasures*	128
Matthew 25:41	*Treasures*	40, 41, 44
Matthew 25:43	*Treasures*	61
Matthew 25:46	*Treasures*	39, 40
Matthew 26:58	*Bypaths*	48
Matthew 26:60	*Bypaths*	97
Matthew 26:67	*Bypaths*	95
Matthew 27:29	*Bypaths*	69
Matthew 27:46	*Bypaths*	87
Matthew 27:46	*Riches*	35, 39
Mark 1:7	*Treasures*	74
Mark 1:8	*Riches*	89
Mark 1:13	*Treasures*	130
Mark 1:25	*Treasures*	72
Mark 3:12	*Treasures*	72
Mark 3:29	*Treasures*	40
Mark 4:36	*Riches*	60
Mark 4:39	*Treasures*	72
Mark 6:13	*Treasures*	123
Mark 6:48	*Nuggets*	42
Mark 7:4	*Treasures*	86
Mark 8:11	*Treasures*	130
Mark 8:30, 32, 33	*Treasures*	72
Mark 9:25	*Treasures*	70, 72
Mark 9:43, 45, 47	*Treasures*	40, 45
Mark 10:2	*Treasures*	130
Mark 10:13	*Treasures*	72
Mark 10:17	*Treasures*	38
Mark 10:25	*Nuggets*	29
Mark 10:30	*Treasures*	38
Mark 10:45	*Nuggets*	26
Mark 10:48	*Treasures*	72

SCRIPTURE	VOLUME	PAGE
Mark 12:15	Treasures	130
Mark 14:13	Treasures	74
Mark 14:71	Nuggets	73
Mark 15:17	Bypaths	69
Mark 16:1	Treasures	123
Luke 1:1-4	Nuggets	54
Luke 1:7	Riches	58
Luke 1:15, 41, 67	Riches	103
Luke 1:33	Treasures	37
Luke 1:55	Treasures	37
Luke 1:68	Treasures	62
Luke 1:78	Treasures	62
Luke 2:1	Bypaths	22
Luke 2:10, 11	Bypaths	23, 27, 32
Luke 2:11	Treasures	32
Luke 2:16	Riches	58
Luke 3:16	Riches	89
Luke 3:19	Treasures	72
Luke 4:1	Riches	103
Luke 4:1	Bypaths	89
Luke 4:2	Treasures	130
Luke 4:2	Nuggets	105
Luke 4:13	Nuggets	28
Luke 4:18	Treasures	124
Luke 4:18	Riches	79
Luke 4:22	Treasures	16
Luke 4:35, 39, 41	Treasures	72
Luke 5:7	Nuggets	22
Luke 5:7	Riches	66, 95
Luke 5:26	Riches	103
Luke 5:39	Treasures	108
Luke 7:14	Treasures	74
Luke 7:16	Treasures	62
Luke 7:33	Nuggets	105
Luke 7:46	Treasures	123
Luke 8:24	Treasures	72
Luke 9:21, 42, 55	Treasures	72
Luke 10:15	Treasures	46
Luke 10:25	Treasures	38
Luke 10:40	Nuggets	98
Luke 11:13	Riches	107
Luke 11:16	Treasures	130
Luke 12:5	Treasures	45
Luke 12:56	Treasures	129
Luke 13:32	Treasures	119
Luke 14:19	Treasures	127, 129
Luke 14:27	Treasures	74

SCRIPTURE	VOLUME	PAGE
Luke 14:32	Bypaths	30
Luke 16:22	Treasures	45
Luke 16:23	Treasures	46
Luke 16:24	Riches	85
Luke 16:24	Treasures	86
Luke 17:3	Treasures	72
Luke 17:9	Treasures	17
Luke 18:15	Treasures	72
Luke 18:18	Treasures	38
Luke 18:25	Nuggets	29
Luke 18:30	Treasures	38
Luke 18:39	Treasures	70, 72
Luke 19:39	Treasures	72
Luke 19:44	Treasures	62
Luke 20:23	Treasures	130
Luke 20:46	Nuggets	62
Luke 22:10	Treasures	74
Luke 22:25	Bypaths	22, 24, 29
Luke 23:2-4	Bypaths	25
Luke 23:40	Treasures	70, 72
Luke 23:43	Treasures	45
Luke 23:46	Treasures	46
Luke 24:39	Nuggets	50, 68
Luke 24:49	Riches	108
John 1:1	Treasures	76
John 1:1	Nuggets	50, 74
John 1:12	Nuggets	94
John 1:12	Riches	92
John 1:14	Nuggets	39
John 1:18	Nuggets	83, 85
John 1:33	Riches	89
John 1:42	Nuggets	55
John 2:5	Bypaths	47
John 2:17	Treasures	16
John 2:24	Nuggets	95
John 3:3, 4	Treasures	21
John 3:7	Nuggets	99
John 3:15	Treasures	38
John 3:16	Treasures	19, 38, 59
John 3:16	Bypaths	32, 36, 71
John 3:16	Nuggets	61, 83, 109
John 3:20	Treasures	71, 72
John 3:31	Nuggets	54
John 3:36	Treasures	38
John 4:1	Treasures	86
John 4:13, 14, 36	Treasures	29, 38
John 4:24	Nuggets	76

SCRIPTURE	VOLUME	PAGE
John 4:34	Riches	57
John 4:42	Bypaths	27
John 5:18	Nuggets	112
John 5:24. 39	Treasures	38
John 6:6	Treasures	127, 130
John 6:27	Treasures	38
John 6:37	Nuggets	114
John 6:37	Treasures	26
John 6:40	Treasures	38
John 6:47	Treasures	38
John 6:51	Treasures	28, 38
John 6:54	Treasures	38
John 6:58	Treasures	38
John 6:66	Treasures	67
John 6:68	Treasures	38
John 6:70	Nuggets	105
John 7:37, 38	Treasures	22, 30
John 7:37, 38	Bypaths	59
John 7:37-39	Nuggets	34, 70, 91
John 7:37, 38	Riches	106
John 8:6	Treasures	130
John 8:9	Treasures	72
John 8:35	Treasures	37
John 8:46	Treasures	71, 72
John 8:51, 52	Treasures	38, 48
John 8:58	Bypaths	24
John 9:35-38	Bypaths	24
John 10:11	Bypaths	38
John 10:27-30	Treasures	28, 38
John 10:30	Bypaths	24
John 10:31	Treasures	74
John 11:2	Treasures	123
John 11:3, 36	Nuggets	62
John 11:26	Treasures	38
John 12:3	Treasures	123
John 12:6	Treasures	74
John 12:25	Treasures	38
John 12:26	Bypaths	47
John 12:34	Treasures	37
John 12:50	Treasures	38
John 13:	Bypaths	84
John 13:5-10	Nuggets	105
John 13:26	Riches	85
John 14:6	Bypaths	97
John 14:6	Nuggets	88
John 14:9	Nuggets	83
John 14:16	Riches	81. 107

SCRIPTURE	VOLUME	PAGE
John 14:17	Riches	108
John 14:16, 17	Nuggets	90
John 14:17, 26	Riches	119
John 14:26	Nuggets	69
John 14:28, 31	Nuggets	61
John 15:7	Treasures	26
John 15:9-13	Nuggets	61
John 15:14, 15	Bypaths	29
John 15:16	Bypaths	42
John 15:20	Bypaths	96
John 16:6	Riches	103
John 16:8	Riches	94
John 16:8	Treasures	71, 72
John 16:12	Treasures	74
John 16:14	Riches	75
John 16:27	Nuggets	63
John 17:2, 3	Treasures	38
John 17:23	Treasures	119
John 18:3	Nuggets	101
John 18:38	Bypaths	97
John 19:2, 5	Bypaths	69
John 19:4. 6	Bypaths	97
John 19:11	Nuggets	54
John 19:12	Bypaths	25
John 19:14, 15	Bypaths	26
John 19:17	Treasures	74
John 19:30	Treasures	120
John 19:30	Nuggets	119
John 20:15	Treasures	74
John 20:27	Bypaths	23
John 21:15-17	Nuggets	63
Acts 1:5	Riches	86, 89
Acts 1:20	Treasures	63
Acts 2:4	Riches	103, 109
Acts 2:8-11	Riches	109
Acts 2:23	Bypaths	40, 99, 100, 102
Acts 2:27, 31	Treasures	46
Acts 2:38	Treasures	76, 77
Acts 2:42	Riches	99
Acts 3:2	Treasures	74
Acts 3:4	Treasures	49
Acts 4:8, 31	Riches	103
Acts 4:27	Treasures	124
Acts 5:9	Treasures	130
Acts 6:1	Treasures	53
Acts 6:1	Bypaths	52
Acts 6:3, 5	Riches	103

SCRIPTURE	VOLUME	PAGE
Acts 6:7	*Bypaths*	42
Acts 6:7	*Riches*	93
Acts 7:23	*Treasures*	62
Acts 7:38	*Riches*	57
Acts 7:55	*Riches*	103
Acts 8:5	*Nuggets*	77
Acts 8:17	*Riches*	109
Acts 9:7	*Nuggets*	40, 41
Acts 9:15	*Treasures*	72
Acts 9:17	*Riches*	103
Acts 9:20	*Nuggets*	111
Acts 10:10	*Nuggets*	107
Acts 10:38	*Treasures*	124
Acts 10:38	*Riches*	79
Acts 10:46	*Riches*	109
Acts 11:16	*Riches*	89
Acts 11:18	*Treasures*	77
Acts 11:24	*Riches*	103
Acts 11:26	*Treasures*	67
Acts 13:9	*Riches*	103
Acts 13:46, 48	*Treasures*	38
Acts 13:52	*Riches*	103
Acts 15:10	*Treasures*	74, 130
Acts 15:14	*Treasures*	62
Acts 15:17	*Nuggets*	43
Acts 15:36	*Treasures*	63
Acts 16:1	*Bypaths*	52
Acts 16:7	*Treasures*	130
Acts 16:31	*Nuggets*	38, 85
Acts 16:33	*Treasures*	86
Acts 17:21	*Riches*	28
Acts 17:28	*Treasures*	53
Acts 17:29	*Treasures*	75
Acts 18:3	*Nuggets*	39
Acts 19:2	*Riches*	109
Acts 19:2	*Nuggets*	96
Acts 19:6	*Riches*	109
Acts 20:28	*Treasures*	49, 63
Acts 20:28	*Bypaths*	38, 75
Acts 21:35	*Treasures*	74
Acts 22:3	*Treasures*	53
Acts 22:3	*Bypaths*	52
Acts 22:9	*Nuggets*	40, 41
Acts 24:6	*Treasures*	130
Acts 25:26	*Bypaths*	23
Acts 26:	*Treasures*	69
Acts 26:5	*Bypaths*	99

SCRIPTURE	VOLUME	PAGE
Romans 1:1	Bypaths	30, 49, 81
Romans 1:1	Treasures	50
Romans 1:16	Nuggets	94, 95
Romans 1:16	Treasures	76
Romans 1:19	Treasures	75
Romans 1:20	Treasures	74, 75
Romans 1:25	Treasures	37
Romans 1:28	Treasures	129, 130
Romans 2:7	Treasures	38
Romans 2:18	Treasures	129
Romans 3:2	Riches	57
Romans 3:23	Nuggets	88
Romans 4:4, 5	Treasures	18
Romans 4:20	Treasures	77
Romans 4:20	Riches	88
Romans 5:2	Nuggets	57
Romans 5:5	Bypaths	36, 71
Romans 5:5	Riches	118
Romans 5:5, 8	Nuggets	61, 109
Romans 5:7-10	Treasures	17, 18
Romans 5:20	Nuggets	80
Romans 5:20	Bypaths	93
Romans 5:20	Treasures	18, 80
Romans 5:21	Treasures	38
Romans 6:1-23	Treasures	17, 38, 51, 79-106
Romans 6:3	Riches	86
Romans 6:12-14	Nuggets	100
Romans 6:13	Bypaths	49
Romans 6:16, 17	Bypaths	49
Romans 6:16-18	Nuggets	45
Romans 6:23	Bypaths	50
Romans 7:15	Nuggets	63
Romans 7:15	Treasures	80
Romans 7:18, 21	Treasures	82, 96
Romans 8:9	Nuggets	97
Romans 8:11	Treasures	90
Romans 8:12	Treasures	96
Romans 8:14	Riches	79
Romans 8:15	Riches	90
Romans 8:16, 26	Riches	118
Romans 8:17	Bypaths	46
Romans 8:26, 27	Nuggets	98
Romans 8:29, 30	Bypaths	99, 105
Romans 9:5	Treasures	37
Romans 11:2	Bypaths	100
Romans 11:6	Treasures	18
Romans 11:36	Treasures	37

SCRIPTURE	VOLUME	PAGE
Romans 12:2	Nuggets	27
Romans 12:2	Treasures	37, 117, 129
Romans 12:2	Riches	68
Romans 12:9	Nuggets	109
Romans 13:4	Bypaths	48
Romans 14:4	Bypaths	47
Romans 14:22	Treasures	129, 130
Romans 15:1	Treasures	74
Romans 15:6	Treasures	32
Romans 15:8	Bypaths	48
Romans 15:30	Bypaths	58
Romans 16:1	Bypaths	48
Romans 16:2	Riches	39
Romans 16:6	Bypaths	49
Romans 16:25	Treasures	37
Romans 16:26	Treasures	37, 38
Romans 16:27	Treasures	37
I Corinthians 1:7	Bypaths	35
I Corinthians 1:9	Riches	98
I Corinthians 1:14	Treasures	86
I Corinthians 1:17	Bypaths	45
I Corinthians 1:20	Riches	68
I Corinthians 1:26-28	Bypaths	49
I Corinthians 1:28	Nuggets	110
I Corinthians 2:1, 4	Riches	14
I Corinthians 2:1-5	Bypaths	44
I Corinthians 2:6	Treasures	114
I Corinthians 2:6	Riches	58, 68
I Corinthians 2:9-16	Riches	13
I Corinthians 2:13	Bypaths	60
I Corinthians 2:14	Treasures	80
I Corinthians 2:15	Treasures	80
I Corinthians 3:1	Treasures	80, 114
I Corinthians 3:1	Riches	58
I Corinthians 3:5	Bypaths	48
I Corinthians 3:9	Riches	101
I Corinthians 3:13	Treasures	128, 129
I Corinthians 4:12	Bypaths	97
I Corinthians 6:3	Nuggets	76
I Corinthians 6:19	Nuggets	91, 97
I Corinthians 6:19	Riches	118
I Corinthians 6:20	Treasures	51
I Corinthians 7:5	Treasures	130
I Corinthians 7:9	Bypaths	53
I Corinthians 7:22, 23	Treasures	50, 51
I Corinthians 8:5, 6	Bypaths	21
I Corinthians 9:7	Bypaths	50

SCRIPTURE   VOLUME   PAGE

I Corinthians 9:17 ....*Nuggets* 38
I Corinthians 9:17 ....*Bypaths* 31
I Corinthians 9:24-27 ....*Bypaths* 52, 56, 62
I Corinthians 9:27 ....*Nuggets* 113
I Corinthians 10:9, 13 ....*Treasures* 130, 131
I Corinthians 10:13 ....*Nuggets* 16
1 Corinthians 10:16 ....*Riches* 99
I Corinthians 11:23 ....*Nuggets* 54
I Corinthians 11:28 ....*Treasures* 129
I Corinthians 12:13 ....*Treasures* 84, 87
I Corinthians 12:13 ....*Riches* 85, 89
I Corinthians 13: ....*Nuggets* 61, 109
I Corinthians 13: ....*Bypaths* 71
I Corinthians 13: ....*Treasures* 59, 111, 117
I Corinthians 14:20 ....*Treasures* 118
I Corinthians 14:24 ....*Treasures* 72
I Corinthians 15:10 ....*Bypaths* 49
I Corinthians 15:23 ....*Bypaths* 35
I Corinthians 15:24 ....*Treasures* 32
I Corinthians 15:44 ....*Nuggets* 48
I Corinthians 15:52 ....*Bypaths* 105
I Corinthians 15:55 ....*Bypaths* 69
I Corinthians 15:55 ....*Treasures* 46, 49
I Corinthians 16:3 ....*Treasures* 129
I Corinthians 16:22 ....*Nuggets* 62
II Corinthians 1:3 ....*Treasures* 32
II Corinthians 1:21 ....*Treasures* 124
II Corinthians 1:21, 22 ....*Riches* 80
II Corinthians 2:11 ....*Nuggets* 29
II Corinthians 2:14 ....*Bypaths* 50, 51
II Corinthians 4:4 ....*Riches* 68
II Corinthians 4:17, 18 ....*Treasures* 38
II Corinthians 5:1 ....*Treasures* 38
II Corinthians 5:20 ....*Bypaths* 30
II Corinthians 5:21 ....*Bypaths* 88
II Corinthians 6:6 ....*Nuggets* 110
II Corinthians 6:14 ....*Riches* 100
II Corinthians 8:1-7 ....*Nuggets* 117
II Corinthians 8:4 ....*Riches* 99
II Corinthians 8:8 ....*Treasures* 129
II Corinthians 8:16 ....*Treasures* 17
II Corinthians 8:22 ....*Treasures* 129
II Corinthians 10:4 ....*Bypaths* 51
II Corinthians 10:5 ....*Nuggets* 18
II Corinthians 11:13-15 ....*Nuggets* 26
II Corinthians 11:31 ....*Treasures* 32, 37
II Corinthians 12:4 ....*Treasures* 45

SCRIPTURE	VOLUME	PAGE
II Corinthians 12:9	*Nuggets*	103
II Corinthians 12:9	*Treasures*	119
II Corinthians 13:5	*Treasures*	129, 130
II Corinthians 13:14	*Riches*	96
Galatians 1:4	*Treasures*	32
Galatians 1:5	*Treasures*	37
Galatians 1:6, 7	*Riches*	76
Galatians 1:9	*Nuggets*	73
Galatians 2:7	*Nuggets*	38
Galatians 2:7	*Bypaths*	31
Galatians 2:9	*Riches*	99
Galatians 3:10	*Nuggets*	73
Galatians 3:13	*Treasures*	51
Galatians 3:27	*Riches*	86
Galatians 4:19	*Treasures*	93
Galatians 4:19	*Riches*	74-78
Galatians 5:10	*Treasures*	74
Galatians 5:16, 17	*Nuggets*	17, 34
Galatians 5:16, 17	*Treasures*	95, 97
Galatians 5:22, 23	*Treasures*	60, 95, 97
Galatians 6:1	*Nuggets*	23
Galatians 6:1	*Treasures*	130
Galatians 6:2	*Treasures*	74
Galatians 6:4	*Treasures*	129
Galatians 6:5	*Treasures*	74
Galatians 6:6	*Nuggets*	115
Galatians 6:6	*Riches*	26
Galatians 6:8	*Treasures*	38
Galatians 6:17	*Treasures*	73, 74
Galatians 6:17	*Riches*	36
Ephesians 1:1	*Nuggets*	71
Ephesians 1:4	*Bypaths*	40, 100
Ephesians 1:14	*Bypaths*	46
Ephesians 1:22, 23	*Nuggets*	24
Ephesians 2:1-3	*Treasures*	51, 102
Ephesians 2:3	*Nuggets*	59
Ephesians 2:8	*Nuggets*	120
Ephesians 2:8	*Bypaths*	103
Ephesians 2:8	*Riches*	95
Ephesians 2:10	*Treasures*	128
Ephesians 3:1-12	*Riches*	97
Ephesians 3:10	*Nuggets*	32
Ephesians 3:11	*Treasures*	37
Ephesians 3:16, 17	*Treasures*	111
Ephesians 3:17	*Nuggets*	22
Ephesians 4:11	*Treasures*	31
Ephesians 4:11	*Riches*	30

SCRIPTURE	VOLUME	PAGE
Ephesians 4:12	Nuggets	35
Ephesians 4:13, 14	Treasures	115
Ephesians 4:13, 14	Riches	58
Ephesians 4:30	Riches	118
Ephesians 5:10	Treasures	129
Ephesians 5:11, 13	Treasures	72
Ephesians 5:18	Nuggets	33
Ephesians 5:18	Riches	103, 104
Ephesians 5:20	Treasures	32
Ephesians 5:23, 30	Nuggets	24
Ephesians 5:25	Nuggets	61
Ephesians 6:6	Bypaths	94
Ephesians 6:12	Nuggets	104
Ephesians 6:20	Bypaths	30
Philippians 1:1	Bypaths	48
Philippians 1:1	Treasures	63
Philippians 1:3-5	Treasures	55
Philippians 1:3-5	Riches	97
Philippians 1:3-6	Nuggets	116
Philippians 1:10	Treasures	129
Philippians 1:12	Nuggets	102
Philippians 1:20	Nuggets	46
Philippians 1:21	Treasures	93
Philippians 1:23	Nuggets	39
Philippians 1:23	Treasures	45
Philippians 1:23	Riches	31, 32
Philippians 1:27	Nuggets	65
Philippians 1:27	Bypaths	51, 58
Philippians 1:30	Bypaths	58
Philippians 2:1	Riches	113
Philippians 2:2	Riches	96
Philippians 2:1-4	Treasures	109
Philippians 2:3, 4	Bypaths	80
Philippians 2:5-8	Bypaths	67, 80, 86, 104
Philippians 2:5-8	Treasures	109
Philippians 2:9-11	Bypaths	24
Philippians 2:11, 12	Treasures	83
Philippians 2:12, 13	Nuggets	69, 102, 118
Philippians 2:17	Riches	31
Philippians 3:5	Bypaths	52
Philippians 3:7-10	Riches	98
Philippians 3:7-16	Bypaths	46, 52, 54, 62, 63
Philippians 3:8	Riches	14
Philippians 3:11	Riches	64
Philippians 3:12-15	Treasures	115
Philippians 3:20	Bypaths	51
Philippians 3:20, 21	Nuggets	50, 65, 66

SCRIPTURE	VOLUME	PAGE
Philippians 4:1	Bypaths	63
Philippians 4:2	Bypaths	80
Philippians 4:2, 3	Treasures	109
Philippians 4:3	Bypaths	58
Philippians 4:6	Nuggets	43
Philippians 4:10-12	Nuggets	116
Philippians 4:10-19	Treasures	25, 56, 66
Philippians 4:15	Nuggets	115
Philippians 4:15	Bypaths	47
Philippians 4:17	Bypaths	47
Philippians 4:18	Bypaths	47
Philippians 4:20	Treasures	32, 37
Colossians 1:13	Treasures	87
Colossians 1:15	Nuggets	82
Colossians 1:24	Bypaths	75
Colossians 1:26	Treasures	37
Colossians 1:27	Treasures	93
Colossians 1:28	Treasures	118
Colossians 1:29	Bypaths	58
Colossians 2:1	Bypaths	58
Colossians 2:9	Treasures	75
Colossians 2:15	Bypaths	50, 51
Colossians 3:2	Riches	35
Colossians 3:4	Treasures	38, 92
Colossians 3:4	Nuggets	74
Colossians 3:12-14	Treasures	118
Colossians 4:12	Bypaths	58
Colossians 4:12	Treasures	118
I Thessalonians 1:1	Nuggets	15
I Thessalonians 1:3	Treasures	32
I Thessalonians 1:6	Riches	26
I Thessalonians 2:2	Bypaths	58
I Thessalonians 2:4	Nuggets	38
I Thessalonians 2:4	Bypaths	31
I Thessalonians 2:4	Treasures	129, 130
I Thessalonians 2:19	Bypaths	35, 64
I Thessalonians 3:5	Treasures	130
I Thessalonians 3:11-13	Treasures	32
I Thessalonians 3:13	Bypaths	35
I Thessalonians 4:14	Treasures	49
I Thessalonians 4:15	Nuggets	86
I Thessalonians 4:15	Bypaths	35
I Thessalonians 5:21	Treasures	129
I Thessalonians 5:23	Bypaths	35
I Thessalonians 5:23	Riches	96
II Thessalonians 1:9	Treasures	41
II Thessalonians 2:1	Bypaths	8, 9, 34

SCRIPTURE   VOLUME   PAGE
II Thessalonians 2:7 ....*Nuggets* 86
II Thessalonians 2:10, 11 ....*Riches* 30
II Thessalonians 2:13 ....*Riches* 94
II Thessalonians 3:11 ....*Treasures* 66
I Timothy 1:1 ....*Bypaths* 27
I Timothy 1:11 ....*Nuggets* 38
I Timothy 1:11 ....*Bypaths* 31
I Timothy 1:16 ....*Treasures* 38
I Timothy 1:17 ....*Bypaths* 26
I Timothy 1:17 ....*Treasures* 37
I Timothy 3:1 ....*Bypaths* 38
I Timothy 3:1, 2 ....*Treasures* 63
I Timothy 3:2, 12 ....*Nuggets* 41
I Timothy 3:10 ....*Treasures* 129
I Timothy 4:7, 8 ....*Bypaths* 57
I Timothy 4:10 ....*Bypaths* 27
I Timothy 5:20 ....*Treasures* 72
I Timothy 6:12 ....*Nuggets* 118
I Timothy 6:12 ....*Bypaths* 58
I Timothy 6:12 ....*Treasures* 38
I Timothy 6:15 ....*Bypaths* 26
II Timothy 1:9 ....*Treasures* 37, 38
II Timothy 1:14 ....*Riches* 118
II Timothy 2:3 ....*Treasures* 73
II Timothy 2:3, 4 ....*Bypaths* 50
II Timothy 2:5 ....*Bypaths* 57, 68, 69
II Timothy 2:10 ....*Treasures* 38
II Timothy 2:15 ....*Nuggets* 117
II Timothy 3:15 ....*Bypaths* 31
II Timothy 4:1 ....*Riches* 24, 25
II Timothy 4:2 ....*Treasures* 72
II Timothy 4:2 ....*Riches* 26, 27
II Timothy 4:3, 4 ....*Riches* 28, 29
II Timothy 4:5 ....*Riches* 30
II Timothy 4:6 ....*Riches* 31
II Timothy 4:7 ....*Riches* 32, 33
II Timothy 4:7 ....*Bypaths* 58
II Timothy 4:8 ....*Bypaths* 57, 64
II Timothy 4:8 ....*Riches* 33, 34
II Timothy 4:9 ....*Riches* 34
II Timothy 4:10-12 ....*Riches* 34-36
II Timothy 4:13 ....*Treasures* 61
II Timothy 4:13 ....*Riches* 36, 37
II Timothy 4:14, 15 ....*Riches* 38
II Timothy 4:16 ....*Riches* 39
II Timothy 4:17 ....*Riches* 39, 40
II Timothy 4:18 ....*Treasures* 37

SCRIPTURE	VOLUME	PAGE
II Timothy 4:18	Riches	40, 41
Titus 1:2	Treasures	37, 38
Titus 1:3	Bypaths	28, 31
Titus 1:7	Treasures	63
Titus 1:9	Treasures	72
Titus 1:12	Treasures	54
Titus 1:13	Treasures	72
Titus 2:11, 12	Treasures	18
Titus 2:13	Treasures	33
Titus 2:14	Nuggets	15
Titus 2:14	Treasures	52
Titus 2:15	Treasures	72
Titus 3:5	Nuggets	69
Titus 3:7	Treasures	38
Philemon 16	Bypaths	48
Hebrews 1:1, 2	Nuggets	51
Hebrews 1:7	Nuggets	76
Hebrews 1:8	Treasures	37
Hebrews 1:9	Treasures	124
Hebrews 2:1	Nuggets	20
Hebrews 2:6	Bypaths	38
Hebrews 2:6	Treasures	49, 63
Hebrews 2:7, 9	Bypaths	69
Hebrews 2:9	Treasures	49
Hebrews 2:10	Treasures	119
Hebrews 2:16	Nuggets	77
Hebrews 2:16	Bypaths	111
Hebrews 2:18	Treasures	130
Hebrews 3:5	Bypaths	48
Hebrews 3:7, 8	Nuggets	20
Hebrews 3:9	Treasures	129, 130
Hebrews 4:14-16	Bypaths	29
Hebrews 4:15	Treasures	130
Hebrews 5:6	Treasures	37
Hebrews 5:7	Nuggets	30
Hebrews 5:7	Riches	40
Hebrews 5:9	Treasures	38, 119
Hebrews 5:11	Riches	55, 56, 88
Hebrews 5:12	Riches	56, 57
Hebrews 5:13	Riches	57, 58
Hebrews 5:13, 14	Treasures	114
Hebrews 6:1	Treasures	118
Hebrews 6:1, 2	Riches	59-63
Hebrews 6:2	Treasures	41
Hebrews 6:3	Riches	64
Hebrews 6:4	Riches	65, 66, 67
Hebrews 6:5	Riches	68, 69, 70

SCRIPTURE	VOLUME	PAGE
Hebrews 6:6	*Nuggets*	21
Hebrews 6:6	*Bypaths*	46
Hebrews 6:6	*Riches*	68-70
Hebrews 6:7, 8	*Riches*	70, 71
Hebrews 6:9-12	*Riches*	71-73
Hebrews 6:13	*Nuggets*	73
Hebrews 6:20	*Treasures*	37
Hebrews 7:17	*Treasures*	37
Hebrews 7:19	*Treasures*	119
Hebrews 7:21	*Treasures*	37
Hebrews 7:24	*Treasures*	37
Hebrews 7:28	*Treasures*	37
Hebrews 9:9	*Treasures*	119
Hebrews 9:10	*Treasures*	86
Hebrews 9:10	*Riches*	63
Hebrews 9:11	*Treasures*	118
Hebrews 9:12	*Treasures*	38
Hebrews 9:14	*Treasures*	37
Hebrews 9:16, 17	*Bypaths*	46
Hebrews 9:27	*Nuggets*	77
Hebrews 10:1	*Treasures*	119, 120
Hebrews 10:19, 20	*Nuggets*	89
Hebrews 10:26, 29	*Nuggets*	21
Hebrews 11:1	*Bypaths*	18, 19, 45
Hebrews 11:9	*Nuggets*	39
Hebrews 11:17, 37	*Treasures*	130, 131
Hebrews 12:1, 2	*Bypaths*	55, 58
Hebrews 12:5	*Treasures*	72
Hebrews 12:23	*Nuggets*	76
Hebrews 12:23	*Treasures*	119, 120
Hebrews 13:5	*Treasures*	25
Hebrews 13:5	*Riches*	35, 39
Hebrews 13:8	*Treasures*	37
Hebrews 13:12	*Nuggets*	57
Hebrews 13:20	*Treasures*	37
Hebrews 13:21	*Treasures*	37
James 1:2	*Treasures*	131
James 1:4	*Treasures*	118
James 1:12	*Bypaths*	65
James 1:12	*Treasures*	131
James 1:13, 14	*Treasures*	130, 131
James 1:17	*Nuggets*	54
James 1:17	*Treasures*	118
James 1:25	*Treasures*	118
James 1:27	*Treasures*	63
James 2:9	*Treasures*	72
James 2:19	*Treasures*	120

SCRIPTURE	VOLUME	PAGE
James 2:22	Treasures	120
James 3:2	Treasures	118
James 3:6	Treasures	45
James 3:15, 17	Nuggets	54
James 4:5	Nuggets	34, 91
James 4:5	Bypaths	77
James 4:5	Riches	81
James 5:7	Bypaths	35
James 5:14	Treasures	123
I Peter 1:1, 2	Bypaths	39-43, 100
I Peter 1:2	Nuggets	72
I Peter 1:2	Riches	93
I Peter 1:3	Treasures	20
I Peter 1:7	Bypaths	78
I Peter 1:7	Treasures	129
I Peter 1:8	Bypaths	82
I Peter 1:11	Riches	118
I Peter 1:12	Nuggets	32
I Peter 1:13	Treasures	20
I Peter 1:18	Treasures	52
I Peter 1:20	Bypaths	99
I Peter 1:22	Nuggets	110
I Peter 1:22	Treasures	57
I Peter 2:1-3	Treasures	107
I Peter 2:7	Nuggets	15, 58
I Peter 2:11, 12	Bypaths	36, 39
I Peter 2:12	Treasures	63
I Peter 2:18-25	Bypaths	25, 47, 91-99
I Peter 2:19, 20	Treasures	17
I Peter 2:25	Treasures	63
I Peter 3:1-5	Bypaths	105-109
I Peter 3:15	Nuggets	93
I Peter 3:18	Bypaths	90
I Peter 3:18, 19	Nuggets	75
I Petre 3:19, 20	Treasures	47
I Peter 3:21	Treasures	86
I Peter 4:11	Treasures	37
I Peter 4:12-14	Bypaths	71-80
I Peter 4:16	Treasures	69
I Peter 5:4	Bypaths	67
I Peter 5:7	Nuggets	44
I Peter 5:8	Nuggets	105
I Peter 5:10	Treasures	37, 38
I Peter 5:11	Treasures	37
II Peter 1:1	Treasures	32
II Peter 1:3	Treasures	75
II Peter 1:4	Nuggets	59

SCRIPTURE	VOLUME	PAGE
II Peter 1:4	Treasures	82
II Peter 1:11	Bypaths	28
II Peter 1:11	Treasures	32
II Peter 1:14	Riches	32
II Peter 1:16	Bypaths	35
II Peter 2:1	Treasures	51
II Peter 2:4	Nuggets	76
II Peter 2:4	Bypaths	90
II Peter 2:4	Treasures	47
II Peter 2:17	Treasures	41
II Peter 2:20	Treasures	32
II Peter 3:4, 12	Bypaths	35
II Peter 3:17	Bypaths	99
II Peter 3:18	Treasures	32, 37
I John 1:1	Treasures	48
I John 1:1-3	Nuggets	50, 60, 67, 74
I John 1:2	Treasures	38
I John 1:3	Treasures	111
I John 1:3, 6, 7	Riches	98
I John 1:7	Nuggets	59
I John 1:8	Treasures	82
I John 1:9	Nuggets	24, 107
I John 2:1, 2	Nuggets	25
I John 2:5	Treasures	121
I John 2:15	Nuggets	61
I John 2:20	Treasures	124
I John 2:20, 27	Riches	80, 81
I John 2:25	Treasures	38
I John 2:27	Treasures	124
I John 2:28	Bypaths	35
I John 3:1	Treasures	17
I John 3:2	Bypaths	82, 105
I John 3:2, 3	Nuggets	70
I John 3:15	Treasures	38
I John 3:24	Riches	118
I John 4:1	Treasures	129
I John 4:7-5:3	Nuggets	61
I John 4:8	Bypaths	71
I John 4:12, 17, 18	Treasures	118, 121
I John 4:18	Bypaths	72
I John 5:11, 13, 20	Treasures	38
I John 5:21	Treasures	69
Jude 6	Bypaths	90
Jude 6	Treasures	47
Jude 7	Treasures	41
Jude 9	Treasures	72
Jude 13	Treasures	41

SCRIPTURE	VOLUME	PAGE
Jude 21	Treasures	38
Revelation 1:6, 18	Treasures	37, 46
Revelation 1:8	Bypaths	96
Revelation 1:10	Nuggets	78, 107
Revelation 2:2, 3	Treasures	72, 74, 128, 130
Revelation 2:7	Treasures	45
Revelation 2:10	Bypaths	67, 68
Revelation 2:10	Treasures	130
Revelation 3:10	Treasures	130
Revelation 3:11	Bypaths	68
Revelation 3:14	Nuggets	83
Revelation 3:19	Treasures	72
Revelation 4:4, 10	Bypaths	68
Revelation 4:9, 10	Treasures	37
Revelation 5:9	Treasures	51
Revelation 5:10	Nuggets	42
Revelation 5:13	Treasures	37
Revelation 6:2	Bypaths	68
Revelation 6:8	Treasures	46
Revelation 7:1-8	Treasures	70
Revelation 7:12	Treasures	37
Revelation 9:7	Bypaths	68
Revelation 10:6	Treasures	37
Revelation 11:15	Treasures	37
Revelation 12:3	Bypaths	70
Revelation 13:	Treasures	70
Revelation 13:1-8	Bypaths	34, 70
Revelation 14:9-11	Treasures	42
Revelation 14:14	Bypaths	68
Revelation 15:7	Treasures	37
Revelation 17:10	Bypaths	70
Revelation 17:12, 13	Bypaths	70
Revelation 19:11	Bypaths	68
Revelation 19:12	Bypaths	70
Revelation 19:13	Riches	85
Revelation 19:20	Treasures	44
Revelation 20:2	Nuggets	104, 105
Revelation 20:10	Treasures	40, 43
Revelation 20:13, 14	Treasures	46
Revelation 21:3	Nuggets	39
Revelation 22:15	Treasures	26
Revelation 22:15	Nuggets	62
Revelation 22:17	Nuggets	111
Revelation 22:17	Bypaths	42